D1187381

CHIPS FROM A WILDERNESS LOG

BOOKS BY CALVIN RUTSTRUM

Way of the Wilderness
The New Way of the Wilderness
The Wilderness Cabin
North American Canoe Country
The Wilderness Route Finder
Paradise Below Zero
Greenhorns in the Southwest
Challenge of the Wilderness
Once Upon a Wilderness
The Wilderness Life
Chips from a Wilderness Log

CHIPS FROM A

Drawings by Gary Jones

WILDERNESS LOG

Calvin Rutstrum

STEIN AND DAY/*Publishers*/New York

ACKNOWLEDGMENTS

The author wishes to thank:
Robert Barrett of Duluth, Minnesota, for the photo *Monarch at Dawn* (moose);
Thermograte, Inc., of St. Paul, Minnesota, for the photo of the Thermograte;
Barbara Von Hoffman of St. Louis, Missouri, for the photo of the timber wolves;
Ray Tremblay of the Alaska Fish & Wildlife Service, Anchorage, Alaska, for the photo of the elevated tower cache;
Mrs. Carl Frank of Rochester, Minnesota, for the photo of the geese;
Doubleday & Co., Inc. of New York City for permission to quote "On Lying Awake at Night" from *The Forest,* by Stewart Edward White;
Seattle Historical Society of Seattle, Washington, for permission to quote the famous speech of Chief Seattle.

First published in 1978
Copyright © 1978 by Calvin Rutstrum

ALL RIGHTS RESERVED.

Designed by Tere LoPrete

PRINTED IN THE UNITED STATES OF AMERICA

Stein and Day/*Publishers*/Scarborough House,
Briarcliff Manor, N.Y. 10510

Library of Congress Cataloging in Publication Data
Rutstrum, Calvin.
    Chips from a wilderness log.

      1. Natural history—North America. 2. Outdoor life —North America. I. Title.
QH102.R83   796.5   77-20847
ISBN 0-8128-2433-4

To my wife Florence who gathered up the chips and logged up the contents to give order to a forest jungle.

Contents

CHIPS FROM A WILDERNESS LOG

A Forerunner to the Log Itself

Long accumulated in a wooden soapbox stored in the cache cabin were scribblings, notebooks, clippings, and other miscellany collected over a half century. I hoped this material would help me recall much of a varied wilderness life as I recorded it at the time. During the culling and sorting I tried to determine what would be most pertinent to those who truly love the wilderness and to those whose inclinations may lead them in that direction.

In the cache cabin are stored many pieces of equipment that reflect on that earlier wilderness experience and today's. On the walls hang some tools which, though still useful, have been supplanted by handier innovations. But the passage of time has lent them a value in sentiment that is no less than the one they have lost in relative utility. The adz and broad ax, for example, have largely given way to the chain saw. That short section of gill net that I had so frequently set in the backwaters of wilderness rivers to supplement the food supply has now been outlawed, except in some waters for commerical fishermen. Other items have become nostalgic tokens of the past. Their effects will be found in some of these pages.

The wilderness itself seems wholly unchanged as I look through the open door of the cache cabin: the windblown lake whitecapped; that animated black object on the

3

"The wilderness itself seems wholly unchanged . . ."

opposite shore in the sheltered mouth of the river a young bull moose feeding on lily-pad roots; the forest near and far looming up as challenging and intriguing as ever, give no indication of change. A vast wilderness remains.

As I pored over the contents of the soapbox and glanced through the door at the untamed scene, I realized that there could be no significant chronology in depicting the wilderness as I had seen it. Yesterday was today and, we hope, tomorrow. Nature has a cycle but no time clock.

In our restless industrial world, it seems that the wilderness has to be experienced only transiently by most people, seldom leisurely. On that premise, the format of this book should synchronize well with that hurried, demanding life, for one can pick a "chip" at the beginning, middle, or end with little lost effect, and no worry of broken continuity. You may browse at will. However, you may find some advantage in taking the episodes in order. I wrote them without stress to be read without stress.

If you're young you may find additional value in these pages because of the perspective they accrue from having been written in my eightieth year. About half of that life has been lived in the wilds or its perimeter, the other half in cities or outer-suburbia. My advanced age and dual life-style can suggest to you the advantages of making discriminating choices in your life's values. That's what this book is about—providing you with the clues upon which you can make your choices.

The title of this book could easily have been *Impressions of the Wilds, Experiences of the Wilderness,* or some such; none of which seemed quite as appropriate as *Chips from a Wilderness Log.* Throughout the book you'll find the flavor of the wilderness, while encountering at the same time a number of incidental facets of life in the wilds, and life as it concerns us all.

The episodes vary in length from a single sentence to several pages. In just a very few instances there are brief

5

references to other books of mine. If your interest is sparked in the subject one of these books covers, you can then go into it at greater length. A list of my books appears on page *ii.*

The Glowing Fire

If our so-called civilization strives for many basic things, surely two of them must be neatness and cleanliness. The modern home and office testify to that. Yet, how can one equate the familiar need in the midst of this fastidiousness, for the open fireplace with its ashes, smoke, soot, and bark-littering wood present in the most ostentatious homes? The answer may be too inscrutable to seek.

My wife and I were invited by the family of one of my readers to have dinner and spend an evening at their home—an extravagant structure with swimming pool, landscaped garden, visual projection room, and other such appurtenances. Modernity, order, and artful ornamentation dominated the place. One would have noticed a bit of lint as an obtruding excrescence on the thick carpeting or upholstering, had it been there—but it was not. Knowing the affluence of our host, we expected to dine at a table with silverware, candelabra, and all the epicurean embellishments offered by wealth. This was not to be.

We were seated around a fireplace—the largest of several in the house. Our host brought out a one-by-two-foot, somewhat beat up and smoke-blackened, empty marsh-

Monarch at dawn (COURTESY OF ROBERT BARRETT)

mallow tin in which were several tiers of home-fashioned, gravel-screen trivets. On the trivets, our host laid raw lake trout fillets which had been in a solution of salt water overnight—a solution, he said, heavy enough to float an egg. In the bottom of the can was a mere handful of hickory-wood shavings, the can then closed with a cap cover. Our host then set this assembly into the fireplace on a bed of glowing embers he had raked to one side of the main flame fire.

On the elevated hearth was a large urn of coffee, different kinds of breads, tartar sauce, appetizers, and dessert. A half hour later the marshmallow can was removed from the glowing embers with asbestos gloves, and the smoked trout was served informally.

The whole procedure, I presumed, was a kindly gesture toward my wilderness inclinations.

In my years of wilderness living, I became acquainted with many varieties of smoked fish and meat, but none were any more delectable than the trout that came out of that smoke-blackened marshmallow can. The charring hickory shavings imparted the smoked flavor, the moisture in the fillets themselves supplying sufficient steam to thoroughly cook them.

For a moment, my thoughts drifted away from the sumptuous surroundings. As I told our host, I could easily imagine myself seated around a campfire a hundred miles from the railhead, in the presence of Indian friends, as I had done on many occasions; the forest looming up behind us, the waves of a wilderness lake rhythmically lapping the shore, while we satisfied our hunger with smoked fish after a long day of travel by canoe and portage.

Most people will surround themselves with ostentation if they have enough money, but none of us escapes that elementalism which complements our primitive selves—our link with the north wind and the comfort of the open, wood fire.

8

Though hickory trees are not indigenous to the Far North, I've always been able to put my hands on enough hickory fuel to smoke fish and meat, simply by salvaging the broken hickory ax and other tool handles that people throw away. A handful of shavings can be made with a knife, or, serving just as well, granules can be made with a coarse rasp. A few broken handles supply enough hickory for a whole year of such periodic smokings.

The Ingeniously Inventive Indian

When the foolish attempt to disparage the Native American, wiser heads often remind them that the Indian invented the canoe and the snowshoe.

But the Indian did much more: he invented a way of life. He discovered that he could live in harmony with his environment, something other numerically superior peoples have failed to do. He has spent ages in tune with Nature, and has left the wilderness as undamaged as he found it.

When do we hope to emulate this extraordinary accomplishment?

A Flat Table Top and Rain on the Roof

After about five weeks of canoe travel in upper Ontario—thirty-three overnight camps, to be exact—my partner and I came upon an unoccupied, rough-log, trapper's cabin at a narrows between two lakes, nearly two hundred miles from the railhead. The sleeping bunk was a shallow bin of dry balsam boughs supported by a "bedspring" of slim, springy balsam poles. Apparently here nothing was wasted; the whole of the young trees had been put to use. A rusty, wood-burning, tin camp-stove buckled from heat and use, with an oven, occupied one corner of the cabin. A tabletop supported by the log wall on one long side, and two legs on the outside corners stood in front of a window. It provided the only first truly flat surface on which to set something that we'd enjoyed for five weeks. All we'd had till then were the not very flat surfaces of the Precambrian Shield, and the blades of our canoe paddles. The surface of the table had been fashioned from logs split into halves and then hued with an ax. So expertly had this been done that no part of the table top was rough enough to tilt or spill our beverage cups. Only those who've spent time in the woods can appreciate how much of a luxury this flat surface was.

We had experienced some periodic, heavy rains on the trip up till then, but most of the time we had traveled under a leaden-gray sky. Drizzle prevailed for days at a time without measurable rainfall, though a downpour always threatened. When we landed at the cabin the sun shone through shifting clouds, reflecting an extravagantly spectacular sunset on the water. The day, till then, had been largely sunny, with fleeting, marshmallowlike clouds, and later a few dark ones forecasting what was to come. The additional luxury of not having to pitch a camp, naturally made the stop a leisurely one. We caught a large walleyed pike (called pickerel in Canada) for our supper, slit the fish in two pieces and baked it in the oven of the tin stove. Should rain come from the threatening overcast, we decided to stay several days if necessary until it passed. We quickly became addicted to domestic bliss at this luxurious stop.

We talked about the importance of contrasts and how the luxury of the rude cabin would not have seemed so exquisite had we not unconsciously been weighing its advantages against the rainy weather camps we had just experienced.

Since the oven was small and fully occupied with the walleyed pike, we baked a large, brown-crusted bannock on top of the stove in a skillet—the bannock enriched with dehydrated eggs and milk, and loaded to capacity with blueberries picked earlier at the cabin narrows where they grew in profusion. With coffee, what remained of the bannock would also provide our breakfast.

Night fell calmly but very dark from an increasingly overcast sky. It became clear that we would luxuriate in our newly found abode for days if the rain persisted.

Our sleeping bags rolled out on the amply wide, dry balsam pole and bough bunk, we stretched out without any intention of falling asleep for a while, instead recapping the journey thus far, and conjecturing what it would be like in the weeks ahead. Shortly, we heard a faint rumble of thunder off to the west. Then another closer, and before we'd rested for more than ten minutes, there was a slight patter of rain on the roof—big distinct drops, so sporadic we could count them. Then of a sudden came a downpour. An increasing wind began to thrash the lake.

"We came onto a rough-log trapper's cabin . . ."

Wave upon wave pounded the shore by the momentum of the wind's nearly four-mile sweep. This lasted some fifteen minutes, after which the wind abated, and the rain settled down to a steady all-night symphony on the roof.

I have never truly understood what there is about rain falling on a wilderness cabin roof that gives one such an exquisite feeling of comfort. So intensely pleasant and enduring is the experience that I have constructed our residence here on the St. Croix River, and our cabins in the Canadian wilderness, so that there are no ordinary ceilings, but rather under-roof paneling to allow us to best hear the rain. Psychologically, our enjoyment of the patter is as inexplicable as our attraction to the open fire, and I am willing to leave both that way—unexplained.

Aesthetic Values

A woodsman once told me that one of the most beautiful things he could think of was a pair of snowshoes standing in the snow, the meshes creating a pattern of golden sunlight and shadow by the evening sun. That is, it was the most beautiful until he saw a certain young lady supported by a very shapely pair of legs at a Chicago bus terminal.

A thing of beauty

Prodigious Youth

Perhaps one of the saddest and yet most awe-inspiring moments of my wilderness experience took place in the early 1920s on a portage trail in the Ontario wilderness. My partner and I had been en route about a week into the wilds by canoe.

As we were making a portage around a cascade, we met two Indian youngsters dragging a birchbark canoe over the portage. A girl and a boy; they could not have been more than ten to twelve years old. One on each side of the canoe's bow, handling it with a cross pole fastened to the gunwales, they dragged the stern along the portage trail. What was ingenious about the arrangement was that the canoe's stern itself was not actually dragging on the trail but was suspended in the crotch of a tag-alder sapling in such a manner as to have it slide along like the single leg of a travois—a method used in early Western Indian horse travel. The stem of the sapling sliding on the trail also served as a spring to take the ground undulations and incidental bumps. It was a method I had not seen used before, something these youngsters had learned from their elders.

The story they told was heartrending. They and their parents had come to dangerous rapids. The youngsters and camp equipment were landed at the head of the whitewater so their parents could run the canoe and a heavy load of smoked moose meat through the whitewater. They'd all planned to camp at the foot of the rapids. Apparently the load was too heavy for this stretch of whitewater—perhaps

"Prodigious Youth"

it snagged on a sharp rock, filled and swamped. The
youngsters later saw the canoe floating in the calm water
below the rapids, the paddles not far away.

Night was falling and there was no sign of the parents.
Darkness, coupled with overcast, they said, made it impossible for them to continue searching the canyon.

One can imagine what went on in the minds of these
lone youngsters. Seeing the canoe and paddles floating in
the still waters below, they swam out and recovered them.

17

They continued the search for their parents by canoe along the cataract but failed to find them. Finally, they went to the head of the rapids, and in light loads carried over the camp gear for the night. The canoe had been stove in on its bottom, but not so badly that they couldn't repair it with a bark patch and some pitch removed from another part of the canoe above the waterline. We marveled at this youthful ingenuity.

It would be easy to imagine these youngsters sobbing in terror, feeling helpless about what they should do. But Indian youngsters are taught resourcefulness and stoicism. Even as infants they are left in tikanagans (cradleboards), hung in trees for hours while their parents are out in a blueberry-burning, picking berries, or otherwise engaged.

The youngsters slept under the canoe, and were up at daylight using the canoe to continue the search for their parents. But to no avail. The parents apparently had been battered into unconsciousness in the rapids and drowned. We later ran these rapids with an empty canoe, and realized the hazard of attempting it with a heavy load of moose meat. The lake below the rapids was rather less than a quarter mile long with a barely discernible current. At its far end a waterfall dropped into another whitewater canyon; then a stretch of several more miles of rather fast-running river. It's likely that the parents' bodies had sunk in the small lake, or perhaps they were carried by the current untold miles into the wilderness.

We learned from the youngsters that they had relatives in an Indian reservation about four days' travel toward the railroad. It was now our responsibility to get the children into their hands.

The youngsters told us that they had been living mostly on blueberries and fish for about a week. They had some flour for bannock, too, which they baked. At night they'd set a short piece of gill net at places they knew from their parents' training were likely to be productive. Again we marveled at the capability of these young people.

The youngsters had already made some emotional adjustment since losing their parents. It hadn't occurred to them that they were taking any undue risk in traveling alone over lake, river, and portage at their age. This was their environment, one they trusted.

For my partner and me, it was, of course, a case of our needing to reverse our route to get the youngsters to the reservation. We were well supplied with provisions, some items fortunately that would excite a youngster's appetite. We set up their 7' × 9' canvas wall tent so close to our sail-cloth wedge tent, we were able to use the same tent stakes on one side. Whatever warmth of spirit we could extend to these youngsters seemed important now. Around a camp-fire, we listened attentively to their every word, amazed at their prodigious efforts in the face of tragedy. When they went to bed we told them what we hoped would be an en-couraging bedtime story and gave them a paternally gentle reassuring pat on their backsides. In our own tent we whispered to each other about the miraculous survival be-havior of these youngsters. We had become very fond of them.

Out on the lake a loon called; a light wind whispered in the conifers overhead. All seemed well with the world. But surely all of us there returned to one thought. "Where were the parents now that their youngsters slept alone, except for us two strangers?"

The next morning we had a good breakfast, packed up and started the first day of the journey to the reservation. No matter what we did, the children were eager to help. They knew the location of every portage to the reservation, so that we seldom referred to our map. In fact, if it had not been the sort of situation it was, we would have enjoyed having them with us on the seven weeks of our planned canoe voyage. There was something so elementally adaptive, so harmonious, so admirable in their every movement in those wilds.

Five days later, toward evening, we reached the reservation. About twenty people gathered at the waterfront to hear the story from the youngsters. These children needed affection and they got more than my partner and I were able to give them in the five days of our wilderness travel together. The women, deeply distressed, took over. As they hugged these youngsters warmly, trying to suppress tears, I realized that all of us are much alike, no matter what our background.

The following morning two additional canoes and four Indian men headed north with my partner and me to search for the bodies. Travel was faster on the water and more strenuous on the portages than my partner and I would ordinarily have pursued, so that when the four Indians reached the route the parents and their youngsters had traveled, and the two of us had also been engaged for a day in the search for the bodies, we were glad finally to be on our own again. Yet, we had learned much from these Indians in the days we traveled with them. They seemed to feel obligated to us for bringing out the youngsters and made every effort to demonstrate it with help on camp chores, portaging, and in their general attitude.

Living and traveling with the youngsters for five days was a highly rewarding experience for us, and we made it known to the men that it was one we appreciated and would never forget.

When we arrived back at the reservation after our canoe travel through Ontario and Manitoba, we were warmly received. The bodies of the parents had finally surfaced. They were recovered and given the customary Indian ritual burial.

As we sat around a night campfire at the Indian camp in

the reservation, the two youngsters came over and sat close to us, saying very little. They had missed us as much as we had missed them.

Luxury

Something in the process of getting older—or is it the era of increasing convenience in which we live—causes us to overrefine and overimprove the basic wilderness cabins we build and occupy. In earlier days we appreciated the elementary, the simple, and avoided fastidiousness. H. L. Mencken said that people go camping because they like being dirty. He has a point beyond the facetious: such daintiness can become wearisome. It can enlist you as the sedulous slave to a refinement that does not allow full freedom.

The simple cabin, generally built of logs cut from the nearby forest, or contrived with lumber, stone, or adobe, with a sturdy, properly designed little outhouse back forty feet on a winding trail, served as well as an elaborate structure, except for the phlegmatic or disabled individual. And one could contrive means to take care of the needs of the disabled, too.

In the simple cabin there were no problems of sewage, pollution, upkeep, and devastating taxes. Modernity began and ended with at most a propane refrigerator for preserving meat and other perishables. But even this was not absolutely essential. There were alternative methods.

"The simple cabin . . . served . . ."

The wood-burning stove cost nothing to operate since the forest provided an ample fuel supply, and it paid you a bonus of healthful exercise. Garbage and refuse got burned in the same stove. If you wanted toast you simply sprinkled salt on the clean, hot cast-iron surface of the stove and laid the bread slices on it. The salt prevented the bread from scorching, and it didn't stick to the toast, either. Afterwards you'd brush the salt into the stove and take it out with the ashes, or you'd save it if economy compelled.

Meat from the forest and fish from a lake or river provided a substantial part of the daily fare—today the greatest expense in the food budget. Berries were to be had for the picking. Most provisions, such as flour, rice, sugar, dried fruits, coffee, tea, dried whole milk, and the like came inexpensively in bulk. Jam could be made quickly with maple sugar and either forest-picked berries or dried fruit. For much more information on this you may want to consult other books of mine such as *The New Way of the Wilderness, North American Canoe Country, Paradise Below Zero.*

Now, by comparison, even what passes for simplicity can still be a luxury. Artful living, as in art per se, incontestably has its basis in simplicity.

Eventually we lose our hold on simplicity. The desire to "improve" and complicate becomes insatiable. "Progressing" from piling wood on the floor to putting it in a woodbox exemplifies this urge. When I added my woodbox, I recalled and copied the design used by early homesteaders. It had a convenient top shelf to hold two buckets of water.

We don't have to throw our wood on the floor, but neither need we use up the most precious hours of life for achievements that are hollow. We can presently afford to err on the side of having less, and give ourselves a much better life, where peace of mind and intellectual attainment become the realized goals—not extravagances and affectations.

". . . I added the woodbox . . ."

"Man Bites Dog" Paradox

One of my most incongruous moments was when, through a strange circumstance, I, a descendent of European immigrants, was obliged to teach an adult male Indian in a organized youth camp how to paddle a canoe. I thought at the time about the many Indians who in the wilds had taught me many of its fine points.

Eventide

The approach of evening in the wilderness usually brings with it a calm. The ruffled lake levels off, and a cool, fragrant freshness permeates the forest. From our cabin vantage point we can look an even mile across the lake into the mouth of the North River, and a great many more lake miles to the east and the west. Moose have been frequenting the mouth of the river and we reckon the end of day with their appearance. So silent are the evenings at times that we can hear the moose coming out of the deep forest a full mile away across the water to feed on the roots of lily pads. Periodically they raise and lower their heads into the water as they feed, and seem to keep a vigilant eye on our cabin.

One often hears or reads about "the silent places." Our evenings in the wilds fit that description. Unfailingly, toward evening, a hermit thrush is heard well back in the forest, the intervals between its songs seem to deepen even more the quietude.

From the nearby bay where beaver have built a house, the calm is sometimes broken by the danger-signal whack of a beaver tail against the surface of the water—some creature has apparently disturbed the beaver in its evening foraging.

And the plaintive call of the white-throated sparrow scarcely ever fails to end the day as the white-throat gives forth its last lingering notes before darkness—generally the last sound of day before the night sounds succeed it. Sometimes, however, we do hear the white-throat after dark. It's then that it earns its appellation, the northern wilderness nightingale.

At sundown, a salmon-colored tinge usually touches everything, the lake blending from the cool blues of the day to the warm orange and gold of evening. Sunsets here can be sensationally colorful. It takes moisture to provide a great display, and the North Country has the numerous lakes and rivers to provide by evaporation enough moisture to form beautiful cloud effects.

There is just enough light lingering then for me to split a little kindling wood for an evening fire in the Franklin open fireplace stove and a breakfast fire in the kitchen stove.

Reluctantly, we light a lamp, for this draws the curtain on the last receding tinge of daylight. We hang onto these passing moments as one hangs onto life's time, sad to see it go, for we know all too well that the day just passing is gone forever. There is usually a recap: "We had a good day," we tell each other, and hope that the dawn will promise another. The new day is the beginning of the rest of our lives.

"... the beaver in its evening foraging."

". . . the Franklin open fireplace stove . . ."

Firewood

For days I had been pulling a small one-man toboggan with a load of camp equipment and provisions to reach a cabin camp in the Ontario wilds. A friend was wintering there along a river. All was going well with him except that his biggest problem, he said, was finding enough dry wood in his immediate area for his wood-burning heater.

I was surprised to learn that he, and so many others wintering in the north, did not know that green birch burns well, once a fire with dry wood is well under way. Though he was living in a primarily coniferous forest, a heavy stand of birch that warranted thinning covered the

27

riverbank a short toboggan haul across the ice from his cabin.

An important factor in burning birch green—or drying it for later use—is that the stove lengths must be split to release the moisture from the bark enclosure. Unsplit birchbark traps that moisture within the wood resulting in its quick decay, and destroying the fuel value. One often sees empty tubes of birchbark in the forest; the interior wood itself has decayed completely.

Winter life became a lot more tenable when my host found that he did not have to search far and wide for dry wood, except to kindle fires. He also found it much simpler to keep an all-night fire going when he found how to install a T with a damper as a backdraft in his stovepipe, along with a vent-pipe damper. (See my book *Paradise Below Zero*, for detailed specifications of this double damper arrangement.)

So much attention has been focused on fuel shortages recently that the burning of wood in wilderness cabins and even in conventional dwellings has increased considerably. Here at our cabin camp on the shore of Lake Superior in Canada we are blessed because pulp rafts broken up by storms, as well as common driftwood, distribute an ample wood fuel supply virtually at our door. Years ago such logs were salvaged by pulp companies using powered watercraft. Today labor costs prohibit such salvage operations. That allows the rest of us to stock up for free. At times our rock shore waterfront has been blocked by "runaway" logs. We've made the most of it.

As my wife and I sit eating our breakfast with a magnificent view over the island-studded water, we frequently see glistening, golden wood cylinders shimmering in the sun. They are peeled pulp logs drifting in toward our shore, eight-feet long, from five to ten inches in diameter. We call them "manna on the waters." Our after-breakfast

28

task then is to get out the pike pole and picaroon for the salvage effort. Cut green in the forest and water-soaked from the lake, they get piled up crisscross on our shore to dry—likely not becoming fuel for another year. Once the logs seem dry enough to saw, we cut them into proper lengths and split them for the Franklin open fireplace stove. Then we pile them into what my wife calls a "ramada" (a wood rick). There they dry further. In a few weeks they'll be thoroughly dried and ready to burn, giving off a lively, cheering flame.

When thoroughly dry, these already barked pulp logs are usually used only for starting fires because we have a large supply of birch trees which need thinning. The latter provide the main fire. Birch splits best in subzero temperatures, although it can be split fairly well at any time.

". . . a 'ramada' (a wood rick)."

Some of the larger white spruce logs that float in get ripped into lumber with a special attachment on the chain saw. We use it to make various things that require planks or squared timbers, every now and then, even boards. White spruce is a strong, quality wood; at one time it was even used for airplane propellers. It also makes good canoe paddles.

With a worldwide fuel shortage, the burning of wood gains greater importance. We need to realize that oil, gas, and coal are not renewable. Wood is. We tend to think that forests are being depleted, but wise handling of forests has demonstrated that growth can even exceed demand—a bit of wisdom that has been wanting for decades. Much of forest growth isn't suitable for lumber. The proper removal of secondary growth as firewood lessening the crowding, increases the stand of lumber trees.

A standard cord of hardwood (4′ × 4′ × 8′) is equivalent in fuel value to about 200 U.S. gallons or 166 Imperial gallons of fuel oil or approximately 1 ton of coal. The heating value of a cord of most softwoods is about half that of hardwood.

When you need all-night heating from a wood-burning stove, you can get it in two ways: providing a backdraft in the stovepipe, and by using a stove that is lined with heat-retaining firebrick or fire clay. Both should be used together for greater efficiency. The brick or clay keeps the room warm for hours after the fire has burned out.

In the past, fireplaces haven't been very efficient heating units, but they've recently been made more efficient by the addition of built-in Heatilator systems. Perhaps the greatest advance has been the Thermograte. That device employs a grate made of iron tubes that pick up air at their lower ends, pass it through the wood-fire-heated tubes by convection, and send it hot at the upper ends back into the room.

30

"The Thermograte . . ." (COURTESY OF THERMOGRATE, INC.)

The air-polluting effects of burning wood are minimal. Wood has about one-thirtieth the volume polluting effect of car and other internal combustion engines, determined on an equal fuel value basis. What we see coming from chimneys of wood fires is deceptive. It's not so much smoke as it is water in the form of steam. The particles of carbon which emerge from chimneys venting wood-burning fires are so heavy they settle quickly in the surrounding vegetation. There they are recycled in the growth process; they don't hang in the air fouling your breathing. The residual ash—only about 50 to 100 pounds per ton of wood—can be spread beneficially on a garden.

Tamarack, hemlock, cedar, and spruce contain trapped pockets of moisture which explode when burned, producing firecrackerlike sounds. These tiny explosions can throw sparks. Avoid the hazard by using a screen for your

31

fireplace, and keep a watchful eye on the progress of your campfire to prevent a forest fire.

The tools you need to get wood out of a forest are a three-quarter or full, single or double-bladed ax, a Swede or bow saw, or a chain saw, block and tackle, or "come-along," and a picaroon for convenience in handling long logs. If several people are available, lug hooks or canthooks are a great help, too. For those of you who aren't familiar with some of these items: the right block and tackle will consist of two triple pulleys, a 100-foot length of strong rope strung through the pulleys, and two lengths of light chain—one 3 to 6 feet long, depending on average tree size; another chain 20 feet long, and a set of connecting links for attaching them to trees. This tackle is used to pull over a tree that leans the wrong way too much before felling. Undercutting sometimes suffices for place-felling without the block and tackle pull over. A picaroon is a hooklike point mounted on a full-size, single-bit ax handle. Just as you'd swing an ax, drive the picaroon into the top end of a log, and you'll find the wood much easier to drag. You can, of course, manage a wood supply with only a saw and ax, but you'll exert much more effort than if you have the proper tools.

Tree-felling accidents occur often enough to warrant mentioning a few safety precautions. A tree is undercut on the side you intend to have it fall. This is a deep notch cut into the trunk with a chain saw or ax. If the tree grows perpendicular and the weight of the branches is quite evenly distributed, it will fall on the undercut side. A slight lean may, of course, alter this. It can then be forced to fall on the undercut side if a substantial tension is put on that side with a triple block and tackle attached as high as you can conveniently reach with a ladder, if one is available nearby in a cabin camp. If not, throw a loop over a branch. The tree usually begins to fall before it is completely severed from the stump, and the crackling sound caused by the breaking of this unsevered portion is your cue to step aside. Your escape route should be sufficiently clear so that you will not be hung up in brush or debris. People have died when they've tried to run from a falling tree without knowing what direction the tree would fall.

Remember: If the tree falls in the direction you're running, you're likely not to make it. Depending on the height of the tree, some part of the trunk, and especially the branches, will probably catch you as a deadfall.

When the crackling sound starts, remove your saw, keep your wits about you, and watch which direction the tree is beginning to lean. Once you know, walk—*don't run*—or you may trip and fall. Go to a point at right angles to the direction of the fall. Do not walk to the opposite direction of the fall because when the butt breaks loose as the tree hits the ground, it may be driven backwards and hit you, probably pinning you against another standing tree.

If your chain saw gets stuck as the tree begins to fall, leave it there and step aside until the tree hits the ground. This usually releases it.

You can avoid cutting your legs and feet with a chain saw or ax by always making the cut so that if you miss or pass through the cut portion, your legs or feet are not beyond the cut.

Washing Clothes

I've seen some rather ingenious devices used for washing clothes in the wilderness. When the temperature is about

50° Fahrenheit or colder, clothes can be soaked clean in soap or detergent for a day or two without the risk of souring, and then merely rinsed. A trapper friend of mine places his clothes in a net bag that's hung in the rapids. There they wash clean in ten minutes, he claims. But not, I dare say, by a woman's standards.

I've also seen clothes put in a wooden chest with hot water and soap, the chest anchored with a chain and heavy weight to the lake bottom. Waves tumbled the floating chest to wash the clothes, followed by rinse cycles.

Another woodsman of my acquaintance told me that he hasn't washed clothes or dishes by hand at his camp for years. He simply puts them in a crib which he tows behind his canoe. My wife gave him a polite dressing-down for polluting the lake. He defended himself by replying that he thoroughly wiped the dishes with paper towels or dry caribou moss before lake-cleaning them.

Economy

We have discovered, almost at peril to the human race, that economy of resources should have been practiced early in our industrial and domestic history. When there appeared to be an abundance of everything, economy seemed needless.

We should, for example, have planted seedling trees early to renew forests for today, rather than cut recklessly, as we did. Long before now, new forests of giant trees would have been supplied. But this called for expensive fertilization, so ravage became the choice.

Of course, some forms of economy can be carried to extremes. I once saw an elderly Indian sitting in the opening of his hogan, splitting matches to double their number. The most humorous example of economy was the man who labeled a box, "STRING—Pieces Too Short to Use."

The Futility of Speed

The bush pilot asked an Indian how long it took him to reach his trapping cabin by canoe.

"Four days," was the Indian's reply.

The pilot told the Indian it would take only an hour by pontoon plane.

"Why?" remarked the Indian.

Our infatuation with speed and getting to a destination quickly, often forces us to bypass many of life's most valuable and profound experiences.

A Case of Frustration

It's easy to understand why so many people are deserting the humdrum and unfulfilling establishment vision to seek whatever is in store for them in a chancy world. Frustration induced by the monotony of what passes for "civilized" life seems to have inspired many to opt for new and brighter horizons. Much of my own reader correspondence is with people who feel that way. Their letters often amount to pleas for help. Some of my books have apparently convinced them that I have a solution for those who see escape in a more elemental and natural approach to life. If the term "solution" can be modified to mean aid, then I immodestly confess that I hope my books provide that.

I became especially interested in the case of a man with a high IQ, and two impressive degrees from a leading university. He was an only son of an affluent family. Awash in material goods, he found himself frustrated. He believed that life held out nothing durable worth pursuing. His parents feared a growing psychopathic trend—even possible suicide.

I met him on one of Lake Superior's tumbling trout streams in the upper Midwest. He was sitting on the ground, his back against a white pine tree; he seemed to stare abstractly at the rushing water in the stream below. His fly-casting rod was leaning into a bush, while I, intent upon picking up a trout or two for lunch, almost stumbled over him. Since I was working toward some promising pools I knew, I had not yet wet a line.

I apologized for my accidental intrusion. He scarcely answered me, but in a very subdued tone asked if I wanted some trout. He had three brook trout in a fancy creel. I introduced myself and sat down on the ground near him, uninvited. Conversation did not flow freely. I caught a tone of polite pessimism in whatever he said.

I was living alone at the time in a cabin of my own a hundred yards or so downstream. He was staying with his parents in an exclusive clubhouse, the Nanibojou, four miles down the nearby road. I explored his interest in trout fishing, with little success. However, he did finally agree to have lunch with me at my cabin after we caught one more trout. The alimentary approach is no doubt the most universal way to demonstrate congeniality.

This was a long time ago. I was single and had been something of a vagabond before I acquired a modest cabin. I had very few dollars for my grubstake, but I didn't mind that state of affairs as long as I had my leisure. As I began to prepare the trout on a wood-burning stove, I saw my guest cast fleeting glances at various parts of my "castle." It was modest, indeed, but adequate. Originally it had belonged to a Lake Superior commercial fisherman—a bachelor. The walls were made of square-hewn logs, and overhead on the collar beams was a canoe—an all wood, cedar-strip Peterborough which I'd recently varnished. In a rack made from the branches of that most beautiful woods—diamond willow—were guns, part of my means of livelihood from the nearby forest, full then of wildlife. Near the gun rack I placed my inexpensive bamboo bait-casting rod. He went outside and picked up his own trout rod and reel—luxurious equipment imported from Hardy in England—and placed them with my rod on the rack along with a book of trout flies.

"Leave them there," he said. "You'll have more use for them than I." He apparently had observed the austerity of my own equipment.

I had a rather substantial wall of books, acquired from a

37

second-hand dealer in Minneapolis through quite a novel trade, described at length in my book, *Challenge of the Wilderness.* He peeled a volume from the shelves and skimmed through it while I continued to fry the trout.

Perhaps something in my modest quarters, in the soiled, body-assimilated buckskin shirt that I wore, and the rather substantial library of secondhand books of widely diversified titles, books that I had intentionally placed on the north wall to add insulation, intrigued him. Was he thinking that maybe I had a better grip on life without his affluence? I had prepared a crisp brown bannock on top of the stove to go with the trout, served tea and stewed dry appricots to round out the lunch.

Something in his manner, some vague clue emanating from his pantomime, I don't know just what, led me to believe that there had been a change for the better from his earlier attitude on the trout stream. He ate heartily. When I asked him if he would go to the spring and fetch a bucket of water so that I could wash up the dishes, he reacted very graciously. As I began to wash our lunch dishes, he took a dish towel from a nail, and carefully wiped the tin cups and tin plates from which we had eaten our lunch, protractedly polishing each dish.

As the afternoon drew on, I found that we were building up a relationship of sorts. He insisted that I have dinner with him and his parents at the clubhouse.

His parents sensed that he was suddenly showing more interest in things than usual. I was sure of this when they quietly motioned me aside while their son was out of the room for a few moments. They said that the meeting along the trout stream and subsequent lunch at my cabin had obviously ignited a spark of some kind, just what it was they could not immediately fathom. "You seem to be very good for him," they remarked. "I hope you can help us." They gave me a hurried rundown on what their apprehensions had been.

38

It was very apparent that here was a fellow who needed a more tangibly elemental approach to life, who could forge a link with the wilderness. Since on his own he had gone fishing on the Flute Reed River, he had shown his inclinations. It may just have been that in our association he was beginning to find the more comprehensive wilderness link that he needed. Sometime later he referred to me as a catalyst in his life.

He stayed with me at the cabin through the late summer, fall, and part of the winter. We made a canoe trip through the boundary waters, extending it well up into Ontario and Manitoba. In December we went to Duluth, and at his expense purchased a complete winter camping outfit: custom-made double winter tent, down sleeping units, and parkas, made at considerable cost to him. Another substantial expenditure was incurred when we managed to purchase four fine sled dogs from a professional breeder. The seemingly excessive cost of the dogs and gear merely amused my companion. His source of revenue seemed inexhaustible.

Although I flinched when he paid the bill, to him it seemed no more than if he were buying my lunch. His parents had told me that expense would be no object in helping their son. I had at first tried to borrow or pick up stray sled dogs, as was the custom those days. Then there would be no expense. But December was a bad time of year for that procedure. Sled dogs were either being used on the trapline or were needed locally to haul wood out of the deeper forests, and for other domestic chores. When I mentioned that highly bred sled dogs could be bought for a goodly sum from a breeder, my companion said, "Well, then, that's the solution." When it turned out that the four sled dogs cost about as much as four saddle horses, my usual austerity could scarcely make the adjustment. However, they were large, magnificent, wolfish-looking creatures whose appearance belied their gentle dispositions

39

"... *we made a canoe trip* ..."

and the other well-known qualities that sled dogs should possess: they had good feet, were well furred, especially important as it concerned the ears; and strong. The dogs were supplied with new harnesses, tethering chains, and other equipment.

We stayed in a small cabin, supplied by the breeder, for several days and personally fed the four dogs until they became accustomed to us. All of this I learned was a part of the cost—a sort of package deal—which did not, all told, make the cost of the dogs seem so exorbitant after all. We were well fed and housed. The most memorable part of the whole deal was the instruction that accompanied the "package." The dogs were taken out on several runs with a loaded toboggan. An Indian who worked for the breeder accompanied us and showed us the best methods for driving the dogs. We were given several admonitions, such as "Don't pet them when they are in harness," and other good advice, along with a feeding chart and instructions for medication, if needed.

In Winnipeg we purchased a Peterborough Prospector model toboggan, a supply of winter camp foods; and there we boarded a Canadian National train with our equipment, the dogs tethered in the baggage car. At first we thought we would have some difficulty in getting the crew of the crack transcontinental train to let us off at a remote wilderness river crossing, but the magnificence of our dogs, our picturesque dress, and our general approach to the whole matter seemed to excite as much interest among the train crew as we personally had for the undertaking. The dogs were very unhappy in the baggage car, alone except for the clerk. They set up a wolfish howl now and then in seemingly utter despair.

The train made a convenient stop at the river crossing, the baggage car drawn up to the far side where there was a good descent to the river. Passengers became concerned by

41

the stop. Some peered eagerly through windows while a few others were let out into the snow beside the track to watch. Snowshoes, a Peterborough wilderness type of toboggan, packs of equipment and provisions, along with a sheathed 30-30 Winchester carbine, rested in the snow. The dogs, seeing us well away from the train, tugged at their tethering chains and were almost frantic. When we loosed them from the car—my companion and I each hanging onto two dogs—we had all we could do to hold them; powerful, vibrant animals they were. The temperature hung at about −30° Fahrenheit, −22° Centigrade. The train with its luxurious comfort and fine food soon gained speed down the track and went out of sight on a curve where it skirted a nearby lakeshore. But we didn't miss it. We were on our own, the dogs seemingly as intense as we with the excitement of the coming journey.

Such stops by the Canadian National Railway crews were repeated at a number of points along the railroad right of way in the ensuing years, a courtesy I greatly appreciated.

Daylight being very short in December, and the day well along, we found a good, slightly elevated but protected area on the riverbank to pitch camp. Soon we had a fire going in a wood-burning, Yukon type stove within the tent; and an outdoor open fire nearby with dog food cooking in a large aluminum pail. Comfortably encamped not more than 200 feet from the railroad right of way, we were awakened at night several times by passing freight trains, the dogs protesting with wolflike howls.

When morning came the dogs were raring to go, and so were we. We had slept well, considering the train interruptions and the fact that we lay talking in our down sleeping bags well into the night. It didn't matter because nights are too long to warrant sleeping all of the dark northern December hours.

By now, my companion seemed to have made a substantial adjustment in his attitude. I gave no hint of probing the earlier problem he had before we met. I could readily empathize with the disillusionment he had felt at the prospect of having to pursue a routine urban existence. Life is usually brand-new to youth no matter how many times it has been repeated and its experiences revealed by others. Apparently it hadn't seemed brand new to him. He had no intellectual shortcoming. He was brilliant, and was widely read. He somehow foresaw by comparative projection every day of the future vicariously lived as he observed others' lives and as he might be doing in the succeeding years.

On one of the canoe trips which we had taken the previous summer he told me one morning that he could not understand how it was, no matter how many times he awoke in the wilderness, and how routinely and repetitively we had breakfast and headed out over a wilderness trail, each day seemed to be new, different, promising, and worthwhile. He vividly described the cinematic unfolding of new country as we saw it from day to day, in a wilderness inviolate and magnificent.

It's not easy to account for one individual suffering at the thought of an urban life, while a vast number of others adjust to it. Perhaps the insight that accompanied his extraordinarily high mental ability accounted for it.

One factor appeared to have done more for his adjustment than anything else, although I am not discounting the therapeutic effect of wilderness life per se. On the previous summer canoe trips we had at times considered the advisability of running certain treacherous rapids. One of these on our route, we had been warned, had taken a few lives. It had an enticing, fast, although smooth stretch of water at its beginning where it seemed anybody with a fair knowledge of canoe handling might well run it to avoid the

43

half-mile portage. How could anyone, we questioned, lose his life in such moderately fast water? We beached the loaded canoe and leisurely explored the full length of the rapid on foot. The smooth, fast water proved to be deceptive and a lure. We noticed that its level dropped deeper into a channel. About a quarter-mile downstream, we discovered to our surprise that the river was compressed between two canyon walls, and seemed to fight for freedom of flow in its confinement as it elbowed its way through the fissure, not a waterfall in the common sense of the term, but rather a violent whitewater.

"We can't run it with a load," I warned, "but we might with an empty canoe." The advisability of doing even this seemed doubtful. "It's dangerous," I warned. He left the decision up to me. "What the hell," I said finally, "do we want to live forever? Let's run it."

His response was just an amused smile. Having spoken with his parents, I wondered just then if he did not consider that it would solve his problems if he didn't make it. We carried the packs over the portage and went back to launch the canoe. "Now," I said, "is the time to change your mind." Again he smiled, and this time *he* said, "What the hell, do we want to live forever?"

In camp, the night after the run through the canyon, we reflected on the satisfaction of success. "I suppose," I said, "it's the successful meeting of any imposing challenge, no matter what it is, that makes life worthwhile." It was the first remark that I had made which even remotely intimated that I knew about his earlier condition, but he seemed to suspect nothing. In the final analysis the challenges we faced apparently had the greatest therapeutic effect upon him, and I must add that he faced them admirably.

His answer gave me a great deal of encouragement about his condition. "One might endure anything in that

45

". . . the river was compressed between two canyon walls . . ."

goddamn city," he said, "if a fellow could live like this for a while now and then."

The temperature as we headed up river with the dogs had risen to −15°, making travel a pleasure. It was my friend's first winter trip, and he gave every indication that he felt it an exhilarating experience. Up to this time, the snowfall had been moderate, the snow on the river quite well packed by the winds. Consequently the loaded toboggan was an easy haul for the dogs. In fact it was difficult to hold them back for the first few miles. We didn't stop for a mugup, although we had prepared coffee each morning in a thermos and some lunch for the occasion. On his first day of travel about the time that a mugup might have been considered, the river suddenly widened out into

"Two woodland caribou came out from the far side of one island . . ."

a magnificent lake dotted with islands. We stopped and stared in contemplative amazement. Two woodland caribou came out from the far side of one island, into the open and stood watching us for a moment, then headed into the mainland forest. The dogs became excited and would have been off on a wild chase had we not quickly tipped the loaded toboggan on its side, while both of us threw our weight on it, anchoring our feet into the crusty snow to increase the drag. We had previously planned to do this upon such a contingency. Soon the dogs gave up trying to drag the upset load and finally responded to our commands.

At noon we stopped on what would be in the open water season, a portage trail. Here we built a comforting fire and ate the neglected mid-morning mugup lunch we had saved.

"How," my partner mused, "can a man be so comfortable out here in the subzero wilds? I actually feel warm. Last night I slept as comfortable in the tent as I would have in a heated house, while outside the tent it was eighteen below? This seems incredible." The tent, mentioned earlier, was double with an insulating dead air space between the inner and outer fabrics. A back-draft-controlled fire in the stove poked along slowly throughout the night, just enough heat to take the sharp frosty edge off the subzero night.

For days we traveled between frozen bodies of water on what in summer would be canoe portages, pitching our second camp of the trip at the far end of one. We set up there because we had heard the muffled sound of a waterfall under the ice, and figured that it might be a good place to do some fishing. We'd fish through the ice below the falls. Fish for dog food was what we were seeking, but, of course, we'd eat fish too. The spot proved productive, and we and the dogs had a fish supper.

For almost two weeks of delightful travel the temperature held comfortable from 0 to only −10°. Then, following a snowfall, it began to drop radically. A day later our field thermometer showed −46°, once reaching −52°. We found a sheltered place to camp in a dense grove of balsam not far from what seemed to have been the effects of a summer twister, several hundred trees blown down and dry as a bone. It was fortunate that we arrived at this spot at the time because the temperature hovered from −40° to −50° for almost a week. Wise men do not travel during such temperatures; −30° is a tenable minimum. We took the time to prepare individual balsam bough shelters for the dogs, banking them with snow, except for an entrance way. The dogs, well fed and heavily furred, resisted the cold ably.

Again back on the trail after the layover, we traveled

48

"We found a sheltered place to camp in a dense grove of balsams . . ."

through Canada's wilderness until the middle of January. The effect of the accumulating snow was beginning to tell. Each day now we had to break trail for the dogs, and then they tugged strenuously at their traces. At times over some portages we had to lend our own full strength to pull the toboggan. The deeper the snow, the fewer miles were covered each day.

We reached the railhead about February 1, where we succeeded in flagging down a local wayfreight train that took us to the next passenger train stop. There we boarded a super continental passenger train for Winnipeg. Our first meal in the dining car was at a table with two young

49

women. They were amused and intrigued by our weathered bush costume. They asked where we'd been.

I've never laughed harder than when my partner replied, "Oh, we were just out for a little weekend skiing up a creek!"

At intervals of several years, we met and spent time in the north together. Then many years passed and I lost track of him. I heard once that his parents had passed away and that he had been on a photographic safari in Africa, but I couldn't verify it. Someone believed that he might have died there.

Many years later, a rather distinguished-looking, gray-haired man, well dressed and groomed, with a neatly trimmed moustache and beard, came to our permanent home on the St. Croix River at the tiny village of Marine on St. Croix, Minnesota—an hour's drive from Minneapolis. My wife answered the door. He asked, "Is Cal home?"

My wife called me from my typewriter and said, "There's a gentleman here asking for you. I don't know who he is."

He took the liberty of walking past my wife into my studio room, extended his hand, and said, "What the hell are you trying to do, Cal, live forever?"

Readers' Author Image

With eleven books published, letters from my readers have increased measurably year after year. A cross section of this mail can be characterized as seeking a way of life.

In the earlier years the appeal of the wilderness frontier was so strong that few sought the advice of others for their explorations or for how to live. Most focused on a trade or profession while the intrepid went exploring on their own, preferring to take their chances in unknown country.

Today I find many of my readers searching diligently—their "antennas" probing, often futilely, in an effort to feel out the future. The future carries fascinating uncertainties, but not as challenging as those posed by the early wilderness. Money is needed more than ever, but the all-absorbing quest for it has lost much of its old obsessive appeal.

Today I received a letter from an Appleton, Wisconsin reader—a stranger to me—who began by saying "Thank you for being you." Apparently, to him, people have been too busy to be themselves in an elementary way, seeking rather to drown their individuality in materialism or lose it in the madding crowd.

"I have read three of your books," he went on, "and developed such rapport with you, I must ask if I may visit you."

I think, though, that he would prefer the me he imagines, rather than the genuine article. He seems to be an individual with his own images of what people and things should be. He'd be disappointed to find me an ordinary human, I'm afraid, less than fulfilling his image of what he has pictured me to be through my books. The me that he's read has had the great advantage of editing, while I would have to stand stark and real before him—"unedited."

I once had occasion to interview a famous surgeon in connection with a court case. At the hospital I found him so busy I could be permitted to see him only momentarily, between operations. I'd pictured him as a handsome, impressive figure. Then I missed him twice as he passed me

in the hall, on his way to and from surgery. The fellow I bypassed was a small, slender, unimpressive-looking, somewhat stoop-shouldered individual. He was a brilliant and inspiring personality. He needed no "editing." But few of us can pass that test.

Natural Dispersion

No matter how thoroughly we accept the premise that Nature is ordered, we're sometimes baffled by manifestation of that same Nature where order and logic do not seem to apply. A whole volume could be written on the strange phenomenon of plant dispersion. Take, for example, the wild carrot. Here on Canada's Lake Superior watershed, this giant, which grows to eye level and higher, is found in profusion. Yet it doesn't grow this abundantly anywhere within a thousand miles.

Inorganic phenomena are dispersed too, of course. Aragonite—a six-sided crystal, varying in size from about an inch to six inches—is abundant in New Mexico, and in Aragon, Spain. Soil and climate may seem conducive to the growth of hemlock in Minnesota, but it prefers Michigan, Eastern Canada, and some other areas having about the same climatic conditions as Minnesota. And so it goes in the most mystifying fashion. Nature—how capricious must you be?

"... *into unknown country.*"

"The wild carrot"

A Matter of Morality

What has happened to the high moral standard of earlier days when we left our wilderness cabin door unlocked, the latchstring on the outside, so that the weary wayfarer could make himself at home?

If there was a supply of split wood on hand, the traveler would replenish it before he left; often adding more than he had used, to repay the courtesy of his unknown host.

Today, cabins have to be locked, windows closed with sturdy inside-fastened shutters, and valuables removed to keep them away from sneak thieves. This penalizes the wilderness traveler who'd have treated the cabin and its contents with respect.

I know a trapper who reached his cabin in late fall for winter trapping, only to find that his whole winter's supply of sawed and split wood had been used up by a party of "campers" who spent the summer on his waterfront. They were rounded up from afar by the police and put to work for a month, replenishing the wood supply. They also got the choice of a heavy fine or a jail sentence.

Another trapper left his cabin unlocked for the accommodation of anyone traveling through, and had a number of utility items stolen. Apparently only one canoe party had passed through that area, and when that same group came through the following September, he got to the cabin before them, and with a second witness lay in wait to see if they might be the culprits. Sure enough, the thieves raided the cabin, taking guns, gas lanterns, sleeping bags, and other items. Convicted of breaking-and-entering and possession of stolen property, a heavy jail sentence kept them from making another canoe trip for a long time.

Fortunately, the spineless, thieving element is in the minority in the wilderness areas.

One fall my partner and I reached the cabin of a trapper who'd befriended us the year before. A bit lame, he hobbled to the waterfront when we called out. At once we were concerned about his limp, but he assured us that all was well. He had suffered a severe sprain and had been worried about not getting established for his winter trapping, when two canoes and four men pulled up to his waterfront. They used several days of their one-month canoe trip to get in the winter wood for the trapper, and also put on a new tarpaper roof for him.

Since these men lived near us, we called on them about midwinter. We learned that the trapper had sent beaver pelts to a Minneapolis furrier, requesting that he make beaver caps for the four men.

In a talk that I was invited to give later at a club to which the four belonged, I announced that while these men wore their beaver caps admirably, they also wore even nobler crowns.

Wilderness Therapy

In my fourscore years, much of it spent in the wilds, I've seen enough to conclude that the wilderness can have a therapeutic effect on many illnesses. Many physical and mental afflictions can be alleviated, and sometimes cured by a combination of fresh air, sunshine, exercise, and an absorbing daily interest in some engaging activity. The average city person won't accept that, just as he often disregards well-founded medical advice from a physician. And even the doctor who understands the benefits outdoor activity can bring rarely prescribes it, since he knows most of his patients wouldn't follow that sort of advice. The circumstances compel him to dose with drugs.

I've often wondered why many an overly fat person fears so many things, such as thunderstorms, hurricanes, burglary, car accidents, and plane crashes, when the weight he carries is equivalent to having a cocked pistol held against his head, while riding over a corduroy road. Fat people who get that way by compulsive eating must recognize that incidentally they have a mental problem to overcome: first to know the meaning of appetite addiction, second to know what is meant by imminent danger. To know that they must reduce, requires maturity. To go beyond that and become lean and hard, necessitates less food and lots of outdoor exercise. It demonstrates recognition that life can be extended for a good long time.

When our family physician paid a friendly visit to us one evening, he brought along a colleague of his who had specialized in the study of antibiotics. This, I thought, would be an opportunity to learn what antibiotics I might take along on wilderness journeys—something I could use if I became seriously ill far from a physician.

"Would you suggest some antibiotics I could carry with me in my first-aid kit?" I asked.

"I'm afraid not," he replied.

"Why not?" I urged.

"That's something you wouldn't understand," he said.

"But death or serious complications might be the only alternative," I explained, "since I might not get back to the outside world for medical help."

He did not answer.

As the evening progressed we discussed many aspects of living in the wilderness. I got a feeling though that he was anxious to acquire information but not ready to give any.

Finally we got onto the subject of celestial navigation. I commented that it was good to know that wherever I happened to be on the sea or in the world's wilds, I need never be lost. He retorted (with a little bit of arrogance, I thought), "Do you mean to tell me that if you were dropped in the middle of an African wilderness and you didn't even know that you were on another continent, you could establish your exact position?"

"Yes," I said. "In fact, I could immediately tell that I was in Africa without instrument observations merely by observing the general position of celestial bodies at that time of day or night. I would then make altitude observations with a sextant and fix my exact position."

"How would you go about doing that?" he asked.

"I'm sorry," I said, "but that's something you wouldn't understand."

Evidently he later relented somewhat from his professional arrogance, since my family physician friend sent a prescription to me signed by the antibiotic specialist.

In response I sent him an autographed copy of my book *The Wilderness Route Finder,* which contained the answer to his orientation question.

Communication

With extraordinary modern equipment for fighting forest fires now available, I once asked the chief forester in the region what his most valuable tool was. "First, radio communication." he said, "and second, the airplane." By triangulation radio communicates the position of the fire from tower to plane to the central headquarters. From there fire-fighting equipment is dispatched by whatever avenues and means are available. In remote roadless areas the plane takes over. With an aerial overview of the entire fire, the observer can speak to the firefighters over their walkie-talkies. He can keep them from getting trapped, and can help get the crew into positions to fight salients of fire which are most threatening.

It has often been said that if there were a high degree of communication between peoples, trouble between them and between countries would be greatly lessened; fewer wars would be fought. Misunderstanding is too often the basic cause. It is very likely that if there had been better communication between Indians and whites in the earlier days, the land and resource problems could have been resolved to the advantage of both. But whites have almost always been greedy, and illogical where Indian land rights are concerned. Perhaps communication fails coincidentally with ethical failure.

In the early days of the fur trade, the handicap of little or no communication between Indians and whites set up consequent difficulties. First, there was the language barrier which left both sides building vague presumptions of suspicion and threat. This was partially resolved when

59

some Indians and Europeans learned each other's languages. An interpreter was most valued if he was Indian. In the vanguard of the traders in the west and northwest Indian country he could ameliorate possible threats of conflict and promote trade between members of the fur company and the Indians of the region. It may be significant that there were more Indians who could speak both white man's languages and Indian than whites who had so managed.

While much had been accomplished by the interpreters, there still remained that great barrier of not being able to carry on relationships with Indians by the written word. Indians did, of course, have a sign language. Symbols sufficiently understood by the various tribes were used to communicate among them, but there was no written language in the normal sense of the term. Fur companies occasionally did employ Indians as post managers, but that was rare because of racial discrimination in assigning these jobs.

When communication between Indians and whites was at its worst, an Anglican missionary arrived—a man described by Edgerton Ryerson Young in his book *By Canoe and Dog Team,* published in 1890:

> Without any question, the Rev. James Evans was the grandest and most successful of all our Indian Missionaries. Of him it can be said most emphatically, while others have done well, he excelled them all.

Evans traveled extensively from the north shore of Lake Superior to Lake Athabasca and Great Slave Lake, from Hudson Bay to the Rocky Mountains, carrying on his missionary work. Many clerics were similarly employed and have been forgotten. Even the memory of Evans might not have endured had it not been for his invention of the Cree Syllabic Alphabet, setting forth a concise and unique method for teaching a written language to the Indians, as shown below:

CREE SYLLABIC ALPHABET.

INITIALS.	SYLLABLES.				FINALS.
	ā	e	o	a	·
a	ᐁ	ᐃ	ᐅ	ᐊ	ᐤ ow
wa	ᐁ·	ᐃ·	ᐅ·	ᐊ·	X Christ
pa	ᐯ	ᐱ	ᐳ	ᐸ	ᑊ p
ta	ᑌ	ᑎ	ᑐ	ᑕ	ᐟ t
ka	ᑫ	ᑭ	ᑯ	ᑲ	ᐠ k
cha	ᒉ	ᒋ	ᒍ	ᒐ	ᐦ h
ma	ᒣ	ᒥ	ᒧ	ᒪ	ᒼ m
na	ᓀ	ᓂ	ᓄ	ᓇ	ᐣ n
sa	ᓭ	ᓯ	ᓱ	ᓴ	ᐢ s
ya	ᔦ	ᔨ	ᔪ	ᔭ	ᕑ r

Cree Syllabic Alphabet

Evans traveled successfully through Canada by both birchbark canoe and dog team. Then he built and traveled with a tin canoe. Whenever it was punctured in some rough rapid, he went ashore and repaired it with solder and flux, the iron heated in the embers of a wood fire. His fame spread while his enthusiasm for the Great North Country grew, until one day tragedy struck and seriously marred his life.

He was traveling by canoe on the Nelson River with two Indians, one of them his Indian interpreter, perhaps the most remarkable Indian of his day—a man who could speak almost every Indian language and those of the white man. They saw some ducks ahead and a gun was passed to shoot the ducks for food. The gun was accidently bumped against the gunwale of the canoe, discharged, struck the interpreter in the head, and killed him. Evans devoted much of his remaining life to trying to make amends to the Indian's family. He died quietly on November 23, 1846, while visiting a friend back in England.

On a canoe trip through the Berens River years ago, I found that the manager of the Hudson's Bay Company's post at Pikangicum Little Grand Rapids, east of Lake Winnipeg, was an Indian who conducted the post business using only the Evans syllabic alphabet.

No Trespass

Last October on a hike through the St. Croix River Valley, amid the splendor of the autumn foliage, I crossed through a farmer's woodlot. He came to me angry that I should leisurely walk over his woodlot without permission, and accused me of having no respect for the privacy of others.

I listened to his entire harangue, then quietly told him that I didn't think he would mind my walking through his woods, since he had walked over my adjoining forest river front property and had kept his boat on my St. Croix River waterfrontage nearly five years without asking permission— a favor I was willing to grant gladly. "Why not extend a little happiness to your fellow men?" I said.

Have you ever seen a dog admonished by his master, slink off to his kennel, his tail between his legs?

Is it not a joy to see a sign such as the accompanying illustration? This sign appears on the north shore of Lake Superior. The craftsmanship of the sign is as inspiring as its message.

Will the visiting public have the courtesy to reciprocate this generosity and meet the requests of the owner? We hope so.

". . . the sign is as inspiring as the message it contains."

63

Campcraft

Of the thousands interested in camping, I have found few who did not believe that they were proficient in it. Yet, in over a half century of wilderness travel and living, I've discovered only a few individuals who had acquired real competence.

It's like romance. It's hard to find a man who doesn't believe that he's a great lover, but women will attest that truly romantic men are few indeed.

If only competent campers were legion! Wind, storm, and sleet often stay the camper from his self-appointed tasks, but not often enough to suppress his ego when he ventures out on a sunny day.

The vehemence with which many novice campers hold to their own untried methods over empirically proven ones is amazing. You may get away with criticizing a person's religion, his politics, even his choice of a mate; but question his camping ability and you have violent discord. One might condone the tenderfoot's enthusiasm in one sense, since almost any innovation should be given consideration. But what generally occurs is that novelty prevails over tested methods only because it is new, resulting sometimes in tragedy.

While at my cabin one winter I had a visitor who boasted that his sleeping bag was rated by the manufacturer to $-40°$.

"You mean in a moderately heated tent?" I said. He was offended.

That night the temperature reached $-25°$ with no wind. I suggested that he test his sleeping bag. At 1:30 A.M. he

64

was back in the heated cabin making up his bed in a bunk. I got up and made coffee for a much disillusioned camper. Now it was a time for him to tell me what he'd learned about his sleeping bag, not for me to tell him, "I told you so." *Skepticism* and *testing* are invaluable terms in judging any item.

Just this past week at my cabin on the shore of Lake Superior in Canada, I had a visitor who made it clear to me that he needed no sleeping accommodations within the cabin: he preferred sleeping in a small tent which he'd brought. He spent great praise on his own method and equipment, which seemed impractical by my more than sixty years of camping experience. I was concerned that he failed to properly trench the ground around the tent as a precaution in the event of rain, but said nothing about it. I knew he'd learn the lesson.

It was one of those tents that's not staked to the ground, but has its own spring-metal supports. He had also chosen the impractical sponge pad instead of an air mattress. As night wore on, there was the rumble of thunder, then heavy rain and a high, thrashing wind—a common occurrence there. The unstaked tent wanted to take off, but was partially held down by the weight of the camper on the floor cloth. The tent banged about, keeping the camper awake while the untrenched tent soaked the sponge-rubber pad and thoroughly soaked its owner. He did, however, comfortably spend the remaining part of the night—that is, in the cabin.

Was it essential that we discuss camping equipment and methods the next morning? Perhaps. But I offered no comment and his pride in his "camping ability" did not permit it. There was no discussion. Under the circumstances his most commendable move was to spend the night in the cabin despite his injured pride. His least commendable move was failure to analyze and discuss his

65

problem. He seemed to defend his equipment and methods by maintaining silence.

What he needed was a properly designed tent that could also be staked down, and further secured by parrels.

He needed to trench around the tent.

He needed an air mattress instead of a sponge rubber pad should the trenching prove inadequate in a flash flood. This despite the dealer's claim that it would not absorb water. The air mattress would keep the water from reaching the sleeping bag.

Take, for another example, the question of what canoe to use on a wilderness trip. A wilderness canoe obviously has to carry a heavy load on the long trip and still be light enough to be readily portaged. It must have a seaworthy shape and be sufficiently rugged to stand the tortuous maltreatment of whitewater. Especially, it must have ample displacement so as to ride as high as possible on the water when loaded—not narrowly streamlined as commonly believed to "cut the water." These factors are *not* usually tested, but misleading advertising often leads one to presume that it has been done.

All of these concerns have been worked out, so that there are canoes that take them into account, primarily in the Prospector model. Yet the arguments go on, and the majority of canoes that go into the wilderness are beautiful; but from a practical standpoint they are abominably shaped and do not ride out the rough water or allow, by maximum buoyancy, ease of paddling.

The properly shaped canoe has no fancy, abrupt upturns of bow and stern. See the accompanying photo.

Consider the carrying capacity. It's simple arithmetic. You'll want to maintain a freeboard of at least 6 inches. Divide the load capacity by the weight of the canoe and you'll come up with a very important factor. In a properly designed aluminum canoe, you have a ratio of 1 to 12.6. In

66

The properly shaped canoe and tent

other words, for every pound of canoe weight in the properly shaped canoe, you can carry 12.6 pounds of load. But I emphasize—properly shaped. All the other factors one uses to choose a canoe are equally obvious, and readily proven. Yet I hear endless argument favoring canoes that obviously cannot possibly meet wilderness travel requirements.

Less worthy models will carry much less than 12.6 pounds to each pound of canoe weight, so that the *loaded* canoe, despite its grace of pattern, sags sluggishly in the water. In my book *North American Canoe Country*, these factors are analyzed at length.

The same controversy exists with tents, although it ought to be easy to choose well. Can it withstand heavy winds? Has it a canopylike extension conversion principle so that you can cook under it with an open fire in the rain? Can it be converted so as to reflect heat and aid the drying of clothes in wet, cold weather? Will it keep out insects? Can the mosquito netting be used separately for noonday lunch stops and photography of wildlife from a blind? Can it be converted to use as a double tent with a stove in cold weather? The list of appropriate questions continues and is covered at length in my books *The New Way of the Wilderness, North American Canoe Country,* and *Paradise Below Zero.*

Mosquito-netting tent used separately

Despite these requirements most people choose tents that are nonconvertible rag cells, not suitable for the wide range of weather that can occur in most regions at the change of seasons, or at differing altitudes, from valley to snowline.

Canoe trips that last only a week don't require dehydrated foods to reduce portage weight. Some water-free, quick-to-prepare foods should be included on any trip, of course, but the short trip can be set up to allow you to eat most any staple, even luxurious foods, without encumbering the members with excess weight in toting packs over average portages.

If you're thinking of an extended canoe expedition or backpacking into wilderness country, then, of course you must get down to real water-free food planning. Most provisions you'll take on the average wilderness trip can be found in the supermarket. Some dilettantes affect an esoteric approach; they buy food items from "elite" sources at high cost. Perhaps these people shouldn't be disillusioned if this practice gives them pleasure. Understand, though, that supermarkets can supply the items at one-fourth the cost to the average canoe tripper, and at greater convenience.

Foods packaged for supermarkets should be transferred to suitable waterproof and breakproof containers. You'll find more information on this in my book *The New Way of the Wilderness* and other books of mine. Some jurisdictions don't allow certain kinds of food containers to be taken into wilderness areas. It's best to check before you start out.

Emergency

The day dawned sunny and hot. For mid-June this was normal, except that a cold front from Hudson Bay was soon to collide with a warm front moving up from the southwest. At 4:05 P.M. the collision occurred. The sky, black and threatening, gave just enough warning before the storm broke. Power lines were down and suddenly the mode of life for most in the area dropped back a hundred years. With the electric current off, none of the modern home improvements operated: refrigeration stopped; air conditioners no longer cooled; toilets did not flush; electric stoves cooked no meals; and when the sun went down, light switches did not respond. Neither did the thirsty get water to drink, because pressure tanks supplied no water to the taps.

In this emergency I brought out a portable 3,000-watt generator from our cache cabin. I turned off the master power switch to the electric company source of supply, so as not to create a problem when the power came on again, plugged in the generator, and resumed normal life.

Used to living in the wilds as we are, where there are no buttons to press, we'd have gotten along okay in the blackout even if we hadn't been equipped with the emergency generator. From the gravity flow of our pressure tank, we could draw water from an auxiliary spigot below the tank level, the tap placed there for just such an emergency. Behind a shrub cover, we could dig and use a small pit to "answer nature's call," or use the common commode. We could light candles or use a gasoline mantle lantern if we needed more light. Dinner could be cooked on a portable gasoline camp stove, although we could readily have cooked over an open wood fire with a few dry twigs, something we have done a thousand times in the wilds.

Had the problem occurred in winter, our residence and cabins would be heated with the Franklin type fireplace stove or a regular fireplace. Our fireplace operates in conjuction with two auxiliary units—the Heatilator and the Thermograte for greater efficiency.

But all of the local population wasn't upset by the power outage. As the hours of blackout lengthened, we discovered individuals making adjustments, some with a fine sense of humor. One of these remarked, "Life had been so damned routine this summer, I'm having the time of my life adjusting to the blackout with what I have."

Another said, "I like the challenge. We should have more of them. It pulls people together, makes them better human beings." Some became exasperated, as though they were personally singled out as intentional victims.

Conventional life is not so secure as we'd like to believe. Every household should have a light camp outfit tucked away in a packsack so that when the power buttons no longer respond, you can move out to some natural area to camp and let Mother Nature provide a whole domestic program for you to pursue; in fact, enjoy.

One day after this episode was written, over 20,000 people died in an earthquake in Guatemala; untold numbers were injured. Those who lost their homes were counted in the hundreds of thousands, forced to take up life outdoors with whatever shelters they could provide for themselves. Many made do with nothing. California brush fires annually burn out a number of homes. Fire, hurricanes, earthquakes, war, depressions—the list is well known—all suggest that an indispensable camp outfit be handy for the emergency. (See my book, *The New Way of the Wilderness* for full information on emergency camp equipment and foods.)

71

Predicting Weather

The barometer, said the pessimist (if not also the realist), is an instrument for telling what kind of weather we are having at the moment. On closer study, it does better than that. Satellite photos, prevailing winds, and other such meteorological data, and computer analyses of this information along with electronic communication of this information have made forecasting a science of sorts, but I have often found the need to take such predictions with reservations. While I generally accept the five-day and monthly forecasts, I'm not surprised if Nature's caprice voids these prophetic announcements even the day after they're issued.

With few exceptions, radio and TV weather reporters tell us that the wind is northeasterly, westerly, and so on, which defined by Webster means from or toward the northeast, from or toward the west, and the like. Thus the wind, if we are to accept the predictions, blows from and toward a particular direction at the same time. Some dictionary publishers have apparently struggled with this, for they have tried to pin down the directional data to apply to weather reporting only; that is, if a wind is reported as northeasterly, its actual direction is toward the southwest. If you are now hopelessly confused, so am I. To me—and to most people—if the wind direction is northeasterly, it means just what it says, toward the northeast; but apparently in the vernacular of the weather reporter, the winds blow in the opposite direction.

Even the colloquial sou'wester or nor'easter still make sense, and so do south wind and northeast wind, but a southwesterly or northeasterly wind that goes the other way spins my orientation sense. Doubting my own comprehension of the modern vernacular, I submitted the terms used by weather reporters to a high school class. There was utter confusion. No student, however, misunderstood so direct a statement as that "the wind is from the northeast, or from the south," when it is just that. Another reporter was offended by my polite request to clarify his reporting and continued to stick to rote. His pride injured, he sent me a nasty letter. I answered by telling him that once in Minneapolis we had a very entertaining and successful weather reporter by the name of Hofstrom, who called himself and his wife "HAWF & HAWF." He was finally offered a more lucrative job of weather reporting in Chicago. I told my simmering weather reporters that with the loss of Hawf & Hawf, it was unfortunate that we had to settle for one-eighth. The metaphor had its effect, for I did not hear from him afterward. I'm sure that when he and his employers eventually part company, he will in his last report continue to play the sedulous ape by rote, not submitting to logic or clarification, if rote predictions can sound pretentious.

Disposal and Privy Procedure

Here on the magnificent Canadian shore of Lake Superior, where my wife and I have our hot-weather cabin, we were told by government sanitation authorities that for regulation sewage disposal, we would be required to install a 2,000-gallon tank. It would need to be pumped out at required intervals by a private service. We were also told that we had the choice of an alternate method. We could construct an outhouse—the traditional privy—and provide another pit with a closure lid to dispose of dishwater and other liquids.

Were these last options of privy and pit to save money? Not necessarily. We were advised that they are the most sanitary method yet devised; that had the properly constructed outhouse been retained, much of the pollution problem that plagues the world's water supply would have been greatly minimized. What an encouraging and hopeful legislative improvement Canada is making over those earlier days when the average household was permitted to dump its sewage into freshwater lakes. The United States still defiles its waters.

Many of those old enough to recall the "Chick Sales" outhouse with its crescent-shaped cutout in the door tend to think of it symbolically as an offensive, vertical structure in the shape of a telephone booth, looming up in the backyard. It continually reminds us that we are animals and not the immaculate beings urbane conventionalism promotes to us, and which we avidly try to convey with our inside toilets—toilets that dump outside into our bodies of water. Most of the outhouses were offensive simply because they were poorly constructed and maintained. I have been in some where I feared crashing through the floor and landing in the pit below.

Few of us know the evolution the privy has undergone in recent years. The modern, improved version can be camouflaged, if necessary, by integrating it with a storage shed or garage. It can be partitioned off in one corner and reached by its own modestly hidden doorway at the rear of the building. The pit is curbed at the top with concrete to seal

74

it from insects and rain and to support the wood structure. There is pit ventilation and room ventilation. On a shelf or hanging on a wall is a perfuming deodorizer. But the big innovation in recent years is the use of caustic soda (sodium hydroxide)—a diminisher now packaged commercially, which is emptied into the pit, the empty container dropped in as well, as a safety precaution. It shrinks the fecal matter and renders it odorless. You can thus have a sanitary institution that is superior to the flush toilet. You'll avoid adding pollution to our waters, and you'll keep from your home and bathroom the odors that often escape despite an exhaust fan. Because the product is rather difficult to find, I will, against my usual practice, give the market trade-name and manufacturer: KAYO—The British American Chemical Company Ltd., Barnaby, British Columbia and Regina, Saskatchewan, although I am sure that bulk commercial caustic soda will serve the same purpose. Caustic soda is hazardous; if the dust is inhaled or comes in contact with the skin, it can cause severe irritation.

On a shelf in the modern privy you have a "pitcher and catcher," to use the baseball vernacular. With a pitcher of water and a drain receptacle, you can wash your hands or whatever, and be as fastidious as you choose.

And here's a digression inspired by wilderness living that seems appropriate here. If you have or have not suffered so far from a very common ailment—hemorrhoids—you had better take heed of the following, because just about everybody sooner or later needlessly suffers from piles, more clinically called hemorrhoids, and you will likely not be the exception.

For this purpose, keep a jar of petroleum jelly on the shelf. When you sit down, use your index finger and apply the jelly in and around the rectum, being careful to see that you have a well-trimmed fingernail. If you are squeamish, use a plastic finger-cot or glove. When through, use two

75

applications of toilet paper. Wad up a small amount of toilet paper and wet it as a final swab, then dry with toilet paper. If you have hemorrhoids now, proceed as above and also before leaving, tuck a small portion of tissue into the lower anus, just enough to pinch it there. This has a strong drying and shrinking effect. In a few months, the rectal problem will likely disappear. If you don't have a problem, then the dry and wet process will probably prevent you from ever having one.

You also need to train your evacuation organs. Once trained they will respond by reflex. Don't sit on the seat for long periods straining. Watch an animal. He does it as you should, in one fell swoop. Forget what you can't readily evacuate with the first generous effort, and proceed with the cleaning process. In time you will have trained the bowel to give forth a stool in one single release.

A prominent doctor in a study of the elimination process, discovered that the best position for elimination is that assumed by primitive people, squatting on the ground. This may hark back to thousands of years of evolutionary biological habit. In providing the privy seat, construct it so that you are virtually in a squatting position to simulate the proper primitive position. Thus, there should be a slight recess provided for your heels.

By a frank discussion of a not too pleasant subject, one might avoid surgery, misery, and pollution. A man who had rectal surgery once said that he did not mind the surgery so much, but he was quite put out by the fact that some rectal bandit in the operating room had stolen his "pucker string" (sphincter muscle). His spelling of rectal was somewhat modified from what I have used.

Crisis

There's something in my nature I don't understand. I love crisis, or perhaps the word is adventure. I am more pleased with challenge than with agreement.

I delight in seeing cities so snowbound that cars can't move. People slow down then and feel what is about them. Roaring rapids, even if they have to be laboriously portaged, are far more intriguing on a canoe journey than days of traveling on placid water. Overcast and the rumble of thunder appeals to me more than an abiding starkly blue sky. Yet, benevolence and compassion are clearly preferable to malevolence and violence.

Thanksgiving Day

In 1919 on returning from a wilderness trip, my partner and I had crossed a section of North Country that happened to be low on game and fish because the high Indian population in that region was exhausting the supply. We had run out of food, except for a little flour and some fat. We made, thin, flat, unleavened cakes from water and flour, then fried them brown in fat. Since we had only two days of travel remaining, we were not distressed.

Somehow, in the calculations of our dwindling food supply and time schedule, we had to determine the date in order to catch a steamer that made port only once each week. In the midst of our austere meal it suddenly occurred to us that it was Thanksgiving Day! We did manage to meet the steamer. In the dining room we asked if we could have turkey, although it was not on the menu. The waiter said, "I'll see if there is any left over. It's two days since Thanksgiving, but I'll see what I can do." He brought warmed-over turkey with a smile, and asked, "How can you fellows order turkey two days after Thanksgiving? You must really like turkey."

"Yes," said my partner, "we're simply crazy about it."

The Wilderness Purists and Traditional Methods

The most avid wilderness purist I know derided industry until I reminded him that most of the ingredients of his breakfast, his clothes, his canoe, tent, hunting knife, compass, and the rest were made for him by nine-to-five industry, and five-to-nine farming.

I once received a letter of criticism from a retired sailor purist who thought me negligent in not wrapping the ends of tent and tracking ropes to prevent them from fraying. When I replied that sailors, cowboys, and others haven't wrapped the ends of ropes for fifty years but have dipped them in rubber cement and other compounds to seal the ends, he withdrew his criticism. We need to be brought up to date.

I am reminded of the manager in a research laboratory who on hiring a young prospective research employee warned, "If you can't find some fault with the various experiments we are doing here, and offer a possible solution, you won't last a month."

Occasionally I receive letters from readers of my books who disagree with a piece of advice. If the criticism is valid, I regard it as a welcome contribution for later revision and improvement of the text. Sometimes, though, I get criticism from a person to whom my recommendations only *seem* faulty. Usually the fellow's not even tried my technique. Other comments come from a few who've practiced their mistakes until they've become habit.

Nor can we be happy with the concept that because something is new, it is better. "Put it through the paces," says an old-timer friend of mine. "If it appears to be better than the old, be humble and accept it. If it's not likely to prove better, don't bother with it. It's a waste of time and effort. Especially don't get encumbered with a lot of new gadgets."

A prospector friend of mine criticized the suggestion I made in one of my books that an ax is a precision instrument and should not be left out in the rain. "That's a mistake," he said, "the handle will come loose unless kept moist."

"How," I asked, "does an expert axman like you chop accurately with a handle warped into a banana shape from the rain?" I had tested his vanity. He acquiesced. An ax helve properly set when it is bone dry is not apt to come loose.

79

Literary Critic

To foresee what kind of writing will survive generation after generation would be a monumental, if not impossible, task for modern critics; there's so much being published. But the determination of literary success will more likely lie with the reading public than with the presumed authorities. Nose-counting won't work, though, since a great deal of bad writing often appeals to the masses. Virtually everything published, good and bad, may be preserved for posterity because of the capabilities allowed us by miniaturization and information storage banks.

Last week a professor of literature titillated my ego a bit when he said that the struggle to save the natural environment and the possibility that natural areas might diminish, might well ensure the survival of my writing on wilderness, considerations of intrinsic merit aside. Can it be, I asked, that someday the only inspiration we will have from the wilds will be in the graphic and written form? I doubt it, but I am inclined to believe that past and present wilderness writers will have had a better opportunity to depict the true wilderness than future writers, if most of our natural environment comes to be developed out of its pristine state and much of it developed entirely out of existence.

In my teens I came upon Stewart Edward White's *The Forest*, Dillon Wallace's *The Lure of the Labrador Wild*, and other comparable books which have left a lasting impression upon me. I was especially charmed by White's chapter "On Lying Awake at Night." The remaining chapters in *The Forest* intrigued me but somehow I returned again and again to read "On Lying Awake at Night." I wondered why. Then in the ensuing years I came upon book after book of selected essays in which that chapter was reprinted time and time again.

Could it be, I flattered myself, that I had the eye of a literary critic and could pick the precious from the dross?

I have obtained permission from the publisher to quote the chapter. Since it is short, out of print, and would lose immeasurably by quoting mere passages, or trying to paraphrase the original content, it is quoted here in full. Readers who belong to the fraternity of the wilds will determine why this chapter has been caught up in the fancy of so many publishers, and perhaps will supply a clue as to why it lingered for more than a half century in the core of my mind. Perhaps it may linger in yours.

On Lying Awake at Night

'Who hath lain alone to hear the wild goose cry?'

About once in so often you are due to lie awake at night. Why this is so I have never been able to discover. It apparently comes from no predisposing uneasiness of indigestion, no rashness in the matter of too much tea or tobacco, no excitation of unusual incident or stimulating conversation. In fact, you turn in with the expectation of rather a good night's rest. Almost at once the little noises of the forest grow larger, blend in the hollow bigness of the first drowse; your thoughts drift idly back and forth between reality and dream; when—*snap*—you are broad awake!

Perhaps the reservoir of your vital forces is full to the overflow of a little waste; or perhaps, more subtly, the great Mother insists thus that you enter the temple of her larger mysteries.

For, unlike mere insomnia, lying awake at night in

". . . the voices of the rapids."

the woods is pleasant. The eager, nervous straining for sleep gives way to a delicious indifference. You do not care. Your mind is cradled in an exquisite poppy-suspension of judgment and of thought. Impressions slip vaguely into your consciousness and as vaguely out again. Sometimes they stand stark and naked for your inspection; sometimes they lose themselves in the mist of half-sleep. Always they lay soft velvet fingers on the drowsy imagination, so that in their caressing you feel the vaster spaces from which they have come. Peaceful-brooding your faculties receive. Hearing, sight, smell—all are preternaturally keen to whatever sound and sight and woods perfume is abroad through the night; and yet at the same time active appreciation dozes, so these things lie on it sweet and cloying like fallen rose-leaves.

In such circumstances you will hear what the *voyageurs* call the voices of the rapids. Many people never hear them at all. They speak very soft and low and distinct beneath the steady roar and dashing, beneath even the lesser tinklings and gurglings whose quality superimposes them over the louder sounds. They are like the tear-forms swimming across the field of vision, which disappear so quickly when you concentrate your sight to look at them, and which reappear so magically when again your gaze turns vacant. In the stillness of your hazy half-consciousness they speak; when you bend your attention to listen, they are gone, and only the tumults and the tinklings remain.

But in the moments of their audibility they are very distinct. Just as often an odor will wake all a vanished memory, so these voices, by the force of a large impressionism, suggests whole scenes. Far off are the cling-clang-cling of chimes and the swell-and-fall murmur of a multitude *en fête,* so that subtly you feel the gray old town, with its walls, the crowded marketplace, the decent peasant crowd, the booths, the mellow church building with its bells, the warm, dust-moted sun. Or, in the pauses between the swish-dash-dashings of the waters, sound faint and clear voices singing intermittently, calls, distant notes of laughter, as though many canoes were working against the current—only the flotilla never gets any nearer, nor the voices louder. The *voyageurs* call these mist people the Huntsmen; and look frightened. To each is his vision, according to his experience. The nations of the earth whisper to their exiled sons through the voices of the rapids. Curiously enough, by all reports, they suggest always peaceful scenes—a harvest-field, a street fair, a Sunday morning in a cathedral town, careless travelers—never the turmoils and struggles. Perhaps this is the great Mother's compensation in a harsh mode of life.

Nothing is more fantastically unreal to tell about, nothing more concretely real to experience, than this undernote of the quick water. And when you do lie awake at night, it is always making its unobtrusive appeal. Gradually its hypnotic spell works. The distant chimes ring louder and nearer as you cross the borderland of sleep. And then outside the tent some little woods noise snaps the thread. An owl hoots, a whippoorwill cries, a twig cracks beneath the cautious prowl of some night creature—at once the yellow sunlit French meadows puff away—you are staring at the blurred image of the moon spraying through the texture of your tent.

The voices of the rapids have dropped into the background, as have the dashing noises of the stream. Through the forest is a great silence, but no stillness at all. The whippoorwill swings down and up the short curve of his regular song; over and over an owl says his rapid *whoo, whoo, whoo*. These, with the ceaseless dash of the rapids, are the web on which the night traces her more delicate embroideries of the unexpected. Distant crashes, single and impressive; stealthy footsteps near at hand; the subdued scratching of claws; a faint *sniff! sniff! sniff!* of inquiry; the sudden clear tin-horn *ko-ko-ko-óh* of the little owl; the mournful, long-drawn-out cry of the loon, instinct with the spirit of loneliness; the ethereal call-note of the birds of passage high in the air; a *patter, patter, patter,* among the dead leaves, immediately stilled;

84

and then at the last, from the thicket close at hand, the beautiful silver purity of the white-throated sparrow—the nightingale of the North—trembling with the ecstasy of beauty, as though a shimmering moonbeam had turned to sound; and all the while the blurred figure of the moon mounting to the ridge-line of your tent—these things combine subtly, until at last the great Silence of which they are a part overarches the night and draws you forth to contemplation.

No beverage is more grateful than the cup of spring water you drink at such a time; no moment more refreshing than that in which you look about you at the darkened forest. You have cast from you with the warm blanket the drowsiness of dreams. A coolness, physical and spiritual, bathes you from head to foot. All your senses are keyed to the last vibrations. You hear the littler night prowlers; you glimpse the greater. A faint, searching woods perfume of dampness greets your nostrils. And somehow, mysteriously, in a manner not to be understood, the forces of the world seem in suspense, as though a touch might crystallize infinite possibilities into infinite power and motion. But the touch lacks. The forces hover on the edge of action, unheeding the little noises. In all humbleness and awe, you are a dweller of the Silent Places.

At such a time you will meet with adventures. One night we put fourteen inquisitive porcupines out of camp. Near McGregor's Bay I discovered in the large grass park of my camp-site nine deer, cropping the herbage like so many beautiful ghosts. A friend tells me of a fawn that every night used to sleep outside his tent and within a foot of his head, probably by way of protection against wolves. Its mother had in all likelihood been killed. The instant my friend moved toward the tent opening the little creature would disappear, and it was always gone by earliest daylight. Nocturnal bears in search of pork are not uncommon. But even though your interest meets nothing but the bats and the woods shadows and the stars, that few moments of the sleeping world forces is a psychical experience to be gained in no other way. You cannot know the night by sitting up; she will sit up with you. Only by coming into her presence from the borders of sleep can you meet her face to face in her intimate mood.

The night wind from the river, or from the open spaces of the wilds, chills you after a time. You begin to think of your blankets. In a few moments you roll yourself in their soft wool. Instantly it is morning.

And, strange to say, you have not to pay by going through the day unrefreshed. You may feel like turning in at eight instead of nine, and you may fall asleep with unusual promptitude, but your journey will begin clear-headedly, proceed springily, and end with much in reserve. No languor, no dull headache, no exhaustion, follows your experience. For this once your two hours of sleep have been as effective as nine.

Pure Lard

During World War II fat was in short supply. Much of it was being converted into explosives. The effect of the shortage was felt by many who lived in wilderness areas. Those who found that the caribou migration route had shifted away from them, fell back on the lean diet of snowshoe rabbits, hare, partridge, and ptarmigan. The need for fat as a nutritional supplement to this lean meat diet became serious. When the S.S. *Kenora* was reported to be bringing in a cargo of lard to the wilderness ports of Berens River and Norway House, as well as other ports on Lake Winnipeg, large groups of Indians and whites waited on the docks in anticipation of getting a lard supply.

On a canoe trip into Ontario, I came upon a trapper at his cabin who had just recently put in part of his winter's provisions. He was very concerned about the labels on his lard cans. They read:

PURE LARD

And under this bold claim to the contents, was the following:

CONTAINS: BUTYLATED HYDROXYANISOLE, BUTYLATED HYDROXYTOLUENE & MONOGLYCERIDE CITRATE ADDED. HYDROXYANSOLE BUTYLE, HYDROXYTOLUENE BUTYLE ET CITRATE DE MONOGLYCERIDE AJOUTÉS.

My trapper friend in all seriousness wanted to know if the lard was fit to eat. I had some doubts in the face of these polysyllabic additions. "Some honesty," I added, "might be found in leaving out the modifier 'pure' and simply calling it 'lard.' " But even then it would suffer a bit in the labeling.

In his treatise on the all-meat diet, explorer Vilhjalmur Stefansson has researched the importance of lard in both cold and hot countries. Fat is an essential food supplement; a lean meat diet alone can be a starvation diet. A trapper friend of mine ate a lot of rabbit meat, but rounded out his nutrition with doughnuts.

New York City—Haven of Wildlife

The caption of this chip may have a touch of facetiousness about it, but the recent wilderness chronicles about the existing wildlife in New York City may prove that the title is no joke.

I'll not dwell on the coyotes, wild fowl, song birds, and other fauna that have taken up residence in the habitable parts of the metropolis. This already has had wide documentary coverage. I just want to briefly point out that wildlife species, given half a chance, will not become endangered. We even have boasts from industrialists that a great deal of wildlife thrives on waters which receive cleaned industrial effluents.

One citizen bewailed the fact that people are starving while tons of grain are being fed to New York City songbirds. There obviously is a valid conflict of opinion here and I appreciate the dilemma. But at least I derive pleasure in knowing that metropolitan New Yorkers have not become so urbanly obsessive that they starve their spirits by excluding wildlife.

Grand Portage

Grand Portage is a sixty-four-square-mile Indian reservation on the shore of Lake Superior in the northeast corner of Minnesota—in the area known as Arrowhead Country. It takes its name from the arrowhead shape of the land formed by the Lake Superior shore on one side and the boundary waters between Canada and the United States on the other. At the center of the Grand Portage settlement of Indian cabins and houses, there is a combination trading post and post office, along with a restored building of the famous early fur trade.

At one time in the late 1700s, this tiny wilderness settlement was known in just about every country throughout the world by virtue of the vast amount of fur from over North America that was funneled through Grand Portage, and sold worldwide through the London auctions.

Today Grand Portage has an Indian population of about two hundred and fifty. As one learns the names of the young people, most with mixed white and Indian blood, French voyageur names recall the history of the fur trade.

The 36-foot Montreal canoe, shown elsewhere, was the sort of vessel on which crews of voyageurs transported the 90-pound bales of fur to the East Coast through the Great Lakes and contiguous rivers. They returned with supplies for the Indian trappers: traps, blankets, stroud, tobacco, axes, knives, guns, ammunition, cooking pots, needles, thread, beads, and a vast array of other miscellaneous trade goods—including rum.

Grand Portage was the end of the inland route for the large "Montreal" canoes. Here at Grand Portage smaller canoes, "North" canoes, were used to travel through the thousands of miles of lakes, rivers, and portages north and west of Grand Portage. The smallest birchbark canoe, known as the "Bastard," was used primarily for local trapping.

Once the voyageurs had returned to Grand Portage from their long canoe trips, it's not difficult to understand how they came to meet and marry the attractive Indian girls at Grand Portage—women with both domestic and wilderness skills.

Sixty years ago I had a cabin on the Flute Reed River, about fifteen miles from Grand Portage. I came to know a number of the Indian people. When my wife and I visited Grand Portage recently, we made a number of contacts with the young people, sons and daughters of those I had known earlier—the names of the original voyageurs still as prominent as ever. The young are as proud of their Indian heritage as of the voyageurs. What an interesting dual heritage they possess.

The Federal Government recently made a grant of $3.5 million to Grand Portage for the erection of a hotel, complete with dining room and incidental services, to be operated by the Indians. Since there had been no accommodations for the visiting public, this has been an important complement. Many of us had fears that an imposing industry would come into Grand Portage and reduce its culture to the humdrum of the nine-to-five routine of most communities in the country. Fortunately, the hotel site was chosen about a mile and a half from the actual center of Grand Portage, although still on the reservation. The historical area has thus not been adversely affected. The new hotel accommodations, the cool shore breezes during the hot summer months, and an excellent cross-country ski program in winter, are bringing an influx of tourists that is renewing Grand Portage as a center of life and activity in the region.

The nine-mile portage trail from Lake Superior to the boundary waters canoe routes is still maintained. It has become a great attraction for backpacking campers, who have learned the romantic history of this route to the north. Hiking over the trail, you needn't stretch your imagination to get the feel of what it was like to carry the heavy loads of fur over this portage. It is still a forest trail much the same as it was in those early years, having been brushed out again by the Boy Scouts and maintained since by the Forestry Service and other groups.

In order that I might realize what the trail entailed, about sixty years ago I made a boundary waters canoe trip with a partner, and culminated the trip by making the Grand Portage trek with canoe and packs. The trail at that time was grown over from lack of use since the fur trade. Our portage load was lighter than it had been earlier, since our canoe trip which arced well into Manitoba and Northern Ontario, had taken more than two months. We were thus in our best physical condition for the portage. My partner and I took turns with the canoe and packs, carrying each a half mile in turn.

As we came to a good resting place and had lunch, I tried to picture the tasks of the voyageurs as they labored over the portage. Humorously, as we sat on a rock out-cropping, eating our lunch, I exclaimed loudly, "GRAND PORTAGE!"

The perspiration which had left dirt streaks on our faces, and undried sweat on our shirts, told what the first six of nine unbrushed-out miles had been. The bow of the canoe rested in the crotch of a small tree; that would make it easy to shoulder again for the next half mile stage. We had three miles yet to go. My companion wiped his forehead with a bandanna handkerchief and remarked with a wry, weary smile, "Tell me, what the hell is so grand about this trail?"

Some Grand Portage Indians came over the trail with much lighter loads than we had and offered to help us portage the canoe and packs. But we politely refused and thanked them with a gift of some excess foodstuffs; we explained that we wanted to boast that we had made the full portage. They appeared amused but agreed the trail was rough, then went on at a fast pace, apparently having been over this route a number of times without thought of commendation.

Tall men who carry heavy packs tend to be more afflicted with back trouble than shorter, stockier men. So apparent was this in the early fur trade days that only men of short stocky stature were hired to carry the heavy loads over the portage trails. The tumpline, a head-strap about 2–½ inches wide, to which two lashing straps 1 inch by 8 feet were attached, was used to carry the heavy loads. The wide part of the tumpline was placed across the head; the 8-foot straps bound the load. Fur bales weighed 90 pounds. Two of these bales—a load about the packer's own weight—were carried over the portages by each man.

At the July 1, 1975 celebration of the hotel opening at Grand Portage, my wife and I sat on a soft, luxurious lounge in the hotel lobby waiting to be seated in the dining room by an Indian hostess. I reflected that at about the same spot sixty years ago, I had been cooking an evening meal on this very Lake Superior shore.

The need to preserve some of the old fur-trade traditions is gaining ground. At Grand Portage a modest effort is being made in this direction. Unfortunately, an earlier fair start ended with a fire. The museum burned, along with priceless accumulated artifacts. Something major needs to be done here to preserve the record of that most romantic period. Some effort is being made elsewhere in Minnesota to feature this history, but it is too fragmentary to depict Grand Portage history, nor is it comparable to the grand restoration at Fort William, the alternate fur-trade center, now completed on the Kaministikwia River.

Old Fort William

Although the U. S. Government is doing relatively little to preserve the tradition and culture of the early fur trade at Grand Portage, Minnesota, Canada is restoring and preserving the edifices and culture of Old Fort William. We tend to think, of course, that it was Canada that embraced the fur trade, but much of it spilled down below that border.

A great cooperative tradition between Canada and the United States might have been preserved, had not the United States become revenue hungry and levied a tax on whatever the Hudson's Bay Company and the Northwest Company brought through Grand Portage. It was probably the most regressive tax ever imposed anywhere.

These companies subsequently avoided the tax at Grand Portage by simply abandoning the Grand Portage route into the interior in 1803. They picked up a route on the Canadian side from the mouth of the Kaministikwia River. This new route proved tougher even than the nine-mile Grand Portage out of the Lake Superior watershed, but in view of the tax, it became viable. On the Kaministikwia route one also had to work one's way out of the Lake Superior watershed. The tax made Fort William in Ontario rather than Grand Portage in Minnesota, the intermediate transshipment point between Montreal and the interior of the continent.

In 1881 Fort William was closed, and between 1883 and 1902 all its buildings were demolished to make way for the railways and the grain trade. What a tragedy. As one Canadian recently put it, the wrecked buildings, if they

93

had been reduced to souvenirs the size of match sticks, could have been sold for $100 each, the hinges and latches on the doors for $1,000, while the ground on which they stood was regarded as too priceless to be sold. Now it is a railroad yard.

If in remorse or civic pride, we cannot say—perhaps both—in any event, the vast layout of the demolished fort has been restored on the bank of the Kaministikwia River—a tremendous undertaking of forty-eight buildings plus the functions and the furnishings of every department of the old fur trade. I tried to carefully view the whole restoration in a day and found it impossible.

The project is overwhelming. A high log picket fence surrounds the area. Every department has its tradesmen working an exhibit, and each carries on in the manner and dress of the early days of the trade.

The structural aspect of the buildings compels study of every mortised joint, masterfully doweled together, the imposing beams hand-hewn.

Perhaps the most arresting function from an historical standpoint takes place in the canoe shed—a roomy structure where Montreal, North, and Bastard birchbark canoes are crafted. The tools used are those employed in the early days of the craft, the materials acquired and used in the same fashion. One might assume that these birchbark craft are crudely made but the surprise comes when you see them in all their pristine beauty, skillfully put together. The seams made of spruce roots are clearly the work of master artisans.

Some regard the fur trade's early inroads on the American continent as that of a host of exploiters bent on wringing all the wealth they could from nature. But linked with it was an unforgettable romance, adventure, and consideration for the people employed. In exploitation perhaps it paralleled some of industry today; yet, today's

94

The canoe shed. Note the wood-bending caldron in foreground.

The Montreal canoe skillfully put together, the seams sewed with spruce roots.

The Montreal canoe "in all its pristine beauty . . ."

wilderness industry has little of the charm that was associated with the efforts of those early years. My travel by canoe and dogsled for over a half century in the wilds of Canada allows me to empathize with those who sustained similar rigors in the early wilderness.

A full day at restored Old Fort William instills in one an elementary awareness of every structural and living process of today, and prompts one to wonder what we have achieved in improved living at so great a loss to our environment.

An Unforeseen Gift

Returning from a forty-eight-day canoe trip in Manitoba and Ontario, Canada, my partner and I stopped at the White Dog Indian Reservation, a day's travel from the railroad. We left our excess food with the Indians, keeping just enough for the end of our trip. I tried to have my worn-out, wraparound, Indian-tanned, moosehide moccasins, which I had worn with moccasin rubbers, replaced at the reservation, but was told that moose hides were being tanned though they still had to be smoked.

A lad of about sixteen handed up the excess food items from the canoe to an impressive elderly matriarchal woman. We visited a couple of hours over a pail of tea and some lunch which the woman made. She had such a delightful smile that I remarked to her that it lighted up the whole forest.

When we camped that night after leaving the reservation, I found to my surprise a pair of wraparound moosehide moccasins tucked out of sight under the closing flap of a packsack. The moccasins were a perfect fit.

A Modern Paradox

Some years ago, in Canada's wilderness, I received a written telephone message from a prominent U.S. banker, relayed to me by an Indian in a canoe. I did not know the sender. The message indicated that he would be on the next plane to see me if I would agree to his visit. He had to fly to the nearest commercial airport and then charter a bush, pontoon plane to reach my wife and me at our remote northern Ontario cabin.

The plane came bounding in on a choppy, heavily windblown sea, and taxied to calm water in the lee of our bedrock point. An Indian pilot friend of ours from north of Sioux Lookout wriggled his way out of the cramped cockpit and tossed a line to me. I snubbed it to a steel mooring I had embedded with concrete in the fissures of the bedrock. Then emerged the banker.

He didn't look like a banker—whatever I had presumed that image to be. He looked more like a nattily attired lumberjack. He wore a black and white checkered wool shirt; duckback pants; and footwear that resembled the old, traditional larrigans. He was hatless, with a thick head of hair, dark but streaked with gray—quite a handsome man.

"Before you people get too involved," my wife called out, "come up to the cabin and have some coffee."

The plane soon departed on the return flight to its base without the banker, since I had learned that he could stay over. With an extra pot of coffee, we languished comfortably before the open birch and jackpine fire of a Franklin fireplace stove.

97

Was it a casual visit? He had read all of my books, he explained; in fact, had read and reread them. His mission? Would I, at my leisure, supervise his wilderness training, or at least bring in some trainers to a camp he would pitch, or a rented cabin at the fishing camp on the west end of the lake, who would put him through a routine? For years he had vicariously lived a wilderness life in books, with brief wilderness encounters. The time had come, when theory needed to be applied to practice, if his plans were to be fulfilled.

"How long are you on vacation?" I asked. For here, I presumed, was the usual man of business, who would soon hasten back to the irresistible attraction of making lots of money at whatever sacrifice to the priceless, fleeting hours of life.

I was wrong.

He went on to explain that after more than a year of planning, he had liquidated all of his assets. His accumulated wealth would need no constant attention from him. His total material possessions, except for a footlocker of dress clothes he had left stored in town, were the clothes on his back and a packsack containing a light camp outfit, selected with the knowledge he had gleaned from my books. I had, it was obvious, inescapably acquired a protégé.

"I am," he remarked with a note of modesty, "what you might call a man of some means. I won't insult you, however, by asking for help with you as my employee. What little, or as much attention as you care to devote to me, will be highly appreciated, and whatever remuneration of mutual favor I can give in return, can be your own determination."

I listened rather intently to a narrative which, as he said, he hoped would not bore my wife and me. It did not. It seemed much too paradoxical to us in this industrial age.

He was fifty-nine years old, had raised a family, and some years back had lost his wife in a car accident. There was nothing inspiring in the heart of the city that would give him continued fulfillment in life in his remaining years. The brief encounters with the wilds that he had experienced on vacations left him yearning for more. He saw in the wilderness environment alone, a satisfaction which he could not shake. "There's a very small amount of Cheyenne Indian blood in me," he said, "but it's a very long way back and possibly of no hereditary significance. If it were I suppose that I should be longing for the open country of the West, rather than feel an affinity for this lake, river, and forest wilderness."

The Cheyenne were once woodland Indians, I reminded him.

For two weeks he ran the gamut of wilderness tasks with me and others I had employed. Intently anxious and not yet having learned how to work moderately, perspiration dripped from his chin as he struggled nervously with ax and chain saw with a down-timber clean-up crew. There were calm, placid days of lake travel, but just as many days when whitecaps pitched the canoe like a bucking bronco. There were rapids to run and tents to erect, campfires to be kindled in the rain; short and long portages to be made. Identification of trees and other vegetation along with a knowledge of fauna, needed in a practical approach to wilderness living, consumed many conscientious hours. We shot the sun and stars with a sextant, and after the fundamentals of depending on baselines and coordinates in our travels were learned, I tried experimentally to lose him, with his permission, in the upper country; but he had been too good a student. Once when he had achieved a rather difficult orientation, I said to him, "You must have been a damned good banker." The compliment pleased him.

He had been a consistent volleyball player, he told me,

99

". . . whitecaps pitched the canoe . . ."

"... *portages to be made* ..."

and had spent much time in athletic organizations during his banking career. Conversion to the rigors of the wilderness thus became largely a matter of physical and attitudinal adjustment. He had good reflexes.

At the end of two weeks I suggested that he spend a week alone on a canoe trip in a remote wilderness area. He didn't answer at once, appearing a bit apprehensive, but after some reflection said, "I'll do it." On that trip, as he related on his return, he made some interesting observations. One of these was his reaction to complete solitude. After a few days alone, he said, it seemed that the world he knew on the outside had shrunk to insignificance. In his isolation he saw in retrospect the metropolitan crowd more as an apparition than a memorable reality. In his mind's eye they seemed without purpose, meaning, or importance. "What is the psychology behind this?" he asked. I had no in-depth answer, except to say that perhaps one learns true values best by contrast and objectivity.

He would now, I felt, after a week of complete solitude, know his dependence on mankind. "You were alone a week; how long do you think you could continue that course?" I asked.

"I don't know," he replied. "I think quite a while. There was something wonderful about having night fall on my lone camp and hear only the call of the loon out on the water, the wind rustling in the trees—a strange and profoundly satisfying experience. And at the same time it was fantastic and yet starkly real."

I explained that my request he spend a week alone on a canoe trip was primarily for him to learn the most important lesson of wilderness life—that at least periodically we need the companionship of people to get fulfillment. We need to live on the perimeter of the wilderness and on the perimeter of the crowd, rather than too remotely in the wilds. We should always have the option of

". . . something wonderful about having night fall on my lone camp . . ."

occasional deep wilderness travel, and at times visit the city and its crowds.

I had a plan to suggest but I didn't know if he would subscribe to it. I knew a fine Indian family whom I had admired for years—a trapper with most extraordinary craftsmanship, wilderness skills, and knowledge of natural phenomena; a wife with culture, charm, and wilderness capability; and a young son who seemed to have inherited both of his parents' faculties. His mother had taught him to read when he was five years old, and now at age seven knew, from both textbooks and contact, much of the wilderness life around him. His keen observations of natural phenomena at so young an age often amazed me.

"Since you're a man of considerable means," I confronted the banker, "why don't you buy the most extraordinary wilderness waterfront site you can find, then adopt this Indian family to help you build a log cabin and provide mutual care through the years. You will undoubtedly have the best teachers of the wild and the most congenial companions. I'm sure it will be a priceless arrangement."

The idea really seemed to appeal to him. I relayed a message by pontoon plane to the Indian family. Rather than flying in, they arrived several days later in a canoe with a motor. We visited the remainder of the day, touching tentatively on numerous possibilities for the immediate years ahead. The Indian family and the banker left the following morning in two canoes, one recently acquired by the banker. My wife and I followed them to the first portage, and at the far side saw them all swing out of sight behind a point to live a life that was unpredictable but which held great promise. A year or so later, we visited them on a magnificent waterfront. Here we found that the Indian family and the banker alone had built a spacious log cabin of several rooms that would excite the envy of the

They "had built a spacious log cabin of several rooms . . ."

most skilled craftsman. The harmony we observed between the Indian family and the banker was most gratifying.

As my wife and I headed back over the canoe route to our cabin, I recounted what I had said earlier, "He must have been a damned good banker."

The Grand Feast

I have often wondered if our eagerness to show hospitality in the conventional manner by serving food isn't a crutch. We lean on the technique as a substitute for our poor ability to entertain through conversation.

When Viljhalmur Stefansson and his party had successfully completed the experiment of living for a year on the ice pack, they were met by a ship that had been scheduled to pick them up. The ship's galley had prepared an elaborate feast for the returning party, considering that the hardships of living on ice pack wildlife fare should make this treat a highly welcome one.

When Stefansson met the ship's captain and was told about the prepared feast, epicurean formality had a most devastating setback. Stefansson told the captain that he and his party appreciated the gracious invitation but they were sorry to announce that none of them were hungry.

I hate to think what responsibility would fall on the capability of the average host if a celebrity guest announced on his arrival that he wanted no food and refused to be dined.

Adventure

Viljhalmur Stefansson once said "Adventure is the result of incompetence." As a result, there has been some controversy over the meaning of the term "adventure." The dictionary definition suggests an unusual experience marked by excitement and suspense.

To be able to cope successfully with the wilderness to such a degree that every experience of living and traveling in it is not to be regarded as an adventure, very likely is what Stefansson had in mind.

As to definition, William James, the philosopher, was asked what interpretation he would put on the question of whether one actually walks around a squirrel on the trunk of a tree, if the squirrel continues around on the trunk of the tree, and the observer also walks entirely around the tree. James's answer became one which should apply to many common differences of opinion. He replied, "What does the questioner mean by *around?*" If we carefully use and define our terms there will be less disagreement.

One of the strange aspects of adventure accounts is that high reading interest seems to be generated by narratives of blunder equated with adventurous achievement. Many journeys show a tragic absence of careful preparation in which the members of the parties suffered greatly through the loss of equipment, by weather exposure, abusive damage, carelessness, and the like. The first and simplest way to avoid such loss and pseudo-adventure is to have enough competence to properly pack everything so that it will be protected against the elements and foolish practices. Sometimes we can only presume from much of what we

". . . pack everything so that it will float in an upset . . ."

read that the wilderness travelers knew how to avoid disaster but that the writer considered it important to show needless suffering to make them seem heroic to his readers.

The Watershed

We came upon the sign shown in the accompanying illustration and felt that we must be standing on a pinnacle of the earth, waters draining off the continent as though it were a great shed.

There were no obvious contours to suggesst the change of water direction; yet we soon discovered that the rivers no longer flowed south and east to the Great Lakes, but the other way. A Royal Canadian Mounted Police constable once casually said to me, "I'm going down north this winter on patrol."

The Arctic Watershed sign

THE ARCTIC WATERSHED

North of this watershed all flowing water eventually reaches Hudson Bay, while south of it all watercourses form part of the Great Lakes drainage system. The height of land follows an erratic course of some 1,400 miles across Ontario, ranging from 20 to 175 miles north of Lakes Huron and Superior. This watershed was declared the inland boundary of the tract surrendered to the Crown by Ojibwa Indians in the Robinson Superior Treaties of 1850. It was also widely considered to be the southern limit of Rupert's Land, the vast, ill-defined Hudson's Bay Company territory transferred to Canada in 1870, and it figured prominently in the Ontario-Manitoba boundary dispute of 1883-4.

Erected by the Archaeological and Historic Sites Board,
Department of Public Records and Archives of Ontario

Stream flowing into Lake Superior

Years of canoe travel have made watersheds more
evident to me than the novelty of seeing them illustrated
on maps. Usually a change of watersheds brings on the
long portages, although I have seen a divide that ran
through a lake, with the waters at one end draining north,
and at the other end, south. Obviously, this has to conjure
up a strange picture—waters hang capriciously on the
brink, undecided as to what long journey they will take to
oceans. In one part of Manitoba, we have the Echimamish
River. In Cree that means "The river that flows in two
directions."

Generally, when passing from one watershed to the
other, the route is through small creeks, ponds, and
portages. Often these can be very devious and confusing.

An area of diverging water flow
The "Echimamish—'the river that flows in two directions'"

Where water on the shed seemed to stand still, I have occasionally, when there was no wind, placed a dry leaf on the surface, and watched carefully for a while to see if there was water movement, to learn if I had gone over the hump.

In past years, occasionally one has heard a watershed or divide referred to as a "water parting," but this appellation is now rare. How much better to think of it as a gable-roofed shed, the rain running down two slopes of a roof—on the brink of two oceans.

Since waters can part in even more than two directions, canoe trippers tend to get lost on watersheds more than on other water and land areas.

Sense of Direction

In reaction to an article I once wrote on the sense of direction of wild and domestic animals, I learned the meaning of recalcitrance. I had taken an objective view of animal behavior, noting the errors that are a part of their remarkable innate ability to find their way. A government experiment involving a great number of pigeons showed that most would find their way back from certain distances, but when that distance was increased, error of return increased geometrically. In the experiment, pigeons removed 500 miles from home were found scattered over many parts of the earth.

Most of the letters I received on the sense of direction

capability of animals were claims that the writer's lost pet cat or dog had traveled hundreds of miles to reach home. I resolved to make the test worthwhile to learn the extent of this homing instinct. When I suggested a test, offering to pay the cost of testing such homing capabilities, using their own pets, the confidence of my critics thinned drastically.

To test man's sense of direction a target was placed at the horizon of a Kansas prairie on a heavily overcast, windless day. These precautions prevented those being tested from orienting themselves by using terrain, sun, or wind as possible guides. All the participants were blindfolded after first being allowed to study the target direction, and all of them walked circuitously like a pulled out coiled spring.

When I published the results of my own findings confirming the validity of the Kansas experiments, many people refused to believe me. Yet, whenever I challenged my critics to actual tests, I found no takers.

In a less serious vein, I once discussed the matter of man and animal directional sense with a plane pilot. I had been his passenger on many wilderness charter flights and often commented on his ability to find his way through rain, fog, and darkness. I listened credulously to a story he told. He drew it out so well that I did not know until the punch line came that he was pulling my leg.

A trapper, he facetiously explained, wanted a cat as a pet for company and to keep down the field mouse population in his not-so-rodent-impervious log cabin. The only cat he could come up with had a good home already and seemed reluctant to leave it. About 50 miles out on the trip the pilot opened a window to drop a mail packet in a plastic bag on a lake where another trapper waited to pick it up from his canoe.

As the story went, the cat saw an opportunity to get back home. It leaped out through the window, started spinning

113

its tail like a propeller and beat the pilot back to the point of beginning. "You can't deny," said the pilot with an amused smile, "that cats do have a sense of direction."

Wilderness Access

Whenever I went on foot with a backpack to reach the wilds, I found one of the great access trails a railroad right of way through the wilderness areas. Highways and roads through the wild areas are usually punctuated with settlements. But railroad rights of way, when they traverse wild country, leave on both sides vast, exciting, untrammeled wilderness areas between settlements. North of the Canadian National Railway (CNR), east and west of this railroad from The Pas to Churchill, and east and west on that railroad from North Bay to Moosonee on James Bay, the wilderness stretches uninterruptedly for hundreds of miles. Mountain railroad rights of way also provide this access.

One great advantage of the railroad right-of-way access is that wherever there's an inspiring sight away from the track, you can leave it and travel for awhile along a wilderness river or lakeshore, always with a convenient compass-directional baseline to come back to. The railroad track makes orientation simple and positive.

Of course, you'll come across people wherever the auto makes access convenient. You'll find them on any highway

". . . railroad right-of-way access," to the wilderness

or secondary road. But they're not likely, however, to hike very far along a railroad right of way to reach an otherwise inviolate wilderness area. Another advantage is that you can board a local train to reach a wilderness milepost stop, from which you hike along the track to a wild stretch.

A canoe embarkation point that's accessible by motor vehicle will probably have a lot of people around. Over the first portage you'll lose about 75 percent of them. Over the second portage only the rare individual will be seen, and beyond successive portages, you'll very likely find a silent, inspiring wilderness.

Pontoon and ski-equipped planes make wilderness access easy but costly. Even the big spenders usually remain for very limited periods, "fish their heads off" and are soon gone.

Snowmobiles are seen mostly on cut-out trails, but are few in the remote winter wilderness where winter camping calls for a bit of uncommon know-how. That usually confines the number of snowmobilers to the more competent campers.

Human addiction to passive comfort and a reluctance by most people to travel in remote areas, leaves much of the wilderness unspoiled for those who have the temperament, vigor, and lust to reach it.

Packhorse travel can get you into wild country, although even a small pack train involves costly equipment and wrangler wages, enough to keep this form of travel limited to a few. By their very nature packhorse trains tend to blend naturally with the wilds; they can go plenty of places mechanical means of travel can't reach.

Those who go to the wilderness perimeter by car seldom wander very far from the parking area, so are soon outdistanced by the aggressive, back country backpacker or hiker.

That minority who do get into the deeper wilds consistently are physically lean and hard. They meet happily when they do, and speak a language wholly their own.

Mutual Dependency

It might be said that in my austere earlier wilderness travel I depended on the rich for sponsorship, while the rich depended on my wilderness capability. Something in my approach to the wilds, however, would not allow me to hire myself out as a per diem guide. It could be that this placed me in a rather anomalous position among those who had hoped to employ me. I came to be invited to the homes and social gatherings of affluent families often, I thought, for the entertainment value my wilderness enthusiasm and experience narratives provided.

A beautiful young girl is sometimes advised that it's just as easy to fall in love with a rich man, and I saw the pecuniary merit in occasionally having a rich partner on my journeys into the wilds. It provided a much better status and source of chicken fat than the wages of a guide. What appeared at times to be almost a cold business arrangement proved in several instances the welding of longtime friendships.

On one of these occasions we drove north merely to view the autumn coloring. As we were finishing our dinner with a luscious dessert and coffee in a posh North Country hotel, my host said, "I'd like to have at least one real adventure in my life."

Winter was coming on, so I suggested a dogsled trip in Canada or a canoe trip in the spring.

I was young and rawboned from a wilderness canoe trip in August and September. The autumn coloring by now, October, was beginning to wane. There was a frosty nip in the air, tempting us to get out and flex our legs.

"In mid-December we headed out by dogteam into Ontario's lake and river country."

We got onto a trail that climbed into the hills of the Lake Superior watershed, reaching a rather unusual sugar maple grove, virtually a deciduous island in a vast coniferous forest. I had heard about the squirrels here which were plump from living in season on maple-tree sap, and wanted to see them. We found them to be virtually as fat as little pigs. They would simply bruise the bark and drink the sap.

My companion was puffing quite hard over the uphill trail by the time we reached the summit. "Suppose," I warned, "you have a heart attack on the dogsled trip."

The answer I got was not one I had expected. "Then," he said, "you'll have to make the trip back alone."

"I have a better idea," I suggested. "You diet and get rid

of your excess weight. Then I won't have to 'make the trip back alone.' "

He didn't diet, as I had hoped. In mid-December we headed out by dog team into Ontario's lake and river country. In the first camp on the Winnipeg River he had such a fierce appetite that I advised him to confine his diet wholly to lean meat as a reducing measure. We had taken along some frozen prime beef at the start. The third day out I shot a young white-tailed deer and managed to get my companion to eat primarily the leaner meat. Six days later, as a result of the strict diet, we still had on our dog-sled most of the store provisions we'd started out with, though less of the cereal which had been cooked up with rougher portions of deer meat for the dogs.

On the trail my companion breathed so hard I feared we wouldn't be able to maintain the normal pace of the dogs. It is an unnatural pace—not fast enough for one to jog, and yet too slow to walk and keep up. Whenever I would hold back and ask him if he shouldn't rest, he would say breathless, "Just keep going."' I had to admire his pluck, although I was concerned about maintaining so risky a gait for him this early in the trip.

We were traveling away from the railroad. On about the eighth day I remarked, "This could be the point of no return. If you or I get knocked out one way or another before one of us can get out to the railhead for help, the other might not be able to maintain camp long enough alone in his condition for a rescue."

"Just keep going," he repeated.

In about three weeks I saw what had been so gradual it did not dawn on me until then that his slight paunch had literally disappeared. His plump cheeks had thinned and browned. During that time both of us, and also the dogs, had been living primarily on deer meat and the fish we caught through the ice; although the dogs got cereal, too. The last two weeks we had been covering from 15 to 25 miles per day, whereas earlier it had been only from 5 to 15 miles. I also realized that my companion was not breathing hard over the rough going, and that he broke trail with snowshoes for the dogs oftener and longer than his rather meager earlier attempts.

As I was about to prepare another meal of deer meat, he said abruptly, "I'm so damned hungry for bread, I dream about it at night."

It thus became a day of sudden dietary change. While I had thought at times that he was a bit obstinate about his overexertion, I hadn't realized that he had stuck to the protein diet and the forced travel schedule because he seriously wanted to get rid of the paunch. His obstinacy paid off. I thought about this diligence of his—a quality that had, no doubt, been an asset in making his business a success.

In camp that evening I baked the first bannock of the trip, preparing it in a straight-sided frying pan propped up before an open flash fire. It was a common camp staple recipe: flour, water, salt, a small amount of sugar, shortening, dry buttermilk, and baking powder, baked to a rich brown crust. We put slathers of peanut butter and strawberry jam on it, devouring it with a pail of tea. The choice venison we still had on hand went begging for several days.

From then on we went to a more balanced wilderness diet.

Toward the middle of January we had reached the "Ultima Thule" of our northern journey and headed back for the railhead on a more direct route, reaching it when the snows were getting too deep for routine dogsled travel.

At the station in Winnipeg we found his wife anxiously waiting for us. Her smiling first words on seeing her slimmed-down husband were classic. "For goodness' sake, Cal, where is the rest of my husband?!"

Our Common Mold

Many natural materials which were used to make wilderness gear have in recent years been supplanted by plastics. I have been quite unhappy with most of them. They seem to belong to a style of living where obsolescence is planned. They lack durability. I have been told, however, that plastics of quality and durability do exist, but are too costly for most common items. Wood, steel, copper, aluminum, leather, and natural fibers seem so much more desirable and sound.

There is one plastic, however, if we may call it that, which has always amazed me by its highly estimable properties. It is concrete. A few days ago I mixed one part of Portland cement, two parts of sharp sand, some washed gravel, and water for cabin footings. Today, I am erecting a log cabin on those footings. The mixture of cement, sand, gravel, and water has turned into piers resembling solid rock. Fifty years ago I built a log cabin on similar footings. Today those footings seem as solid and supporting as they were a week after they were poured. If only all common plastics and all human character were like that.

Improved Wilderness Photography

Unless you are well along in years, you won't remember the dollar box camera. It was focused at 18 feet with a fixed diaphragm set at about F/11, so that a near and far picture depth of focus was possible without adjustment. Black-and-white film had sufficient exposure latitude to give a fairly passable print in average light. The camera needed only to be pointed at the subject, the exposure lever clicked, and that was it. In a few days one had some pretty decent commercially finished prints.

The unique simplicity of this method made Eastman a fortune.

Today, amateur wilderness photography can be so involved that the line of demarcation between it and professional photography often vanishes. However, the latest outdoor black-and-white and color photography calls for a technique that is really a lot simpler than we might expect. First you must abandon the old idea of having the sun shine over your shoulder when taking a picture. It is important to keep the sun toward the side or front of the camera, so that the direction of its rays are somewhere in the 180° ahead rather than in the 180° behind. You'll need to shade your lens though to avoid halation. By observing the direction of the shadows you can confirm that most of the unusually good color photographs have this front lighting—color saturation, perspective, and pictorial value being much greater. Sunlight strikes the various facets of the subject and bounces into the camera—the angle of incidence light from any object thus being equal to the angle of reflection.

Consider, too, that when the sun is out in the front 180°, there are likely to be shadows, some so deep that the color film will not record the wide range between shadow detail and highlights with the same exposure. The human eye can observe both the highlights and shadow detail, but the color film latitude cannot span this wide visual spectrum.

What do you do? Go to flash? Yes. Use a modified amount of flash in your most sunlit pictures. In modern photography we call this *fill-in* light. Now the film will span the light range beautifully from bright sun-lighted subjects to deep shadows and give excellent color saturation.

Warning: Do not use too much fill-in light. Use just enough to give detail in the shadows, otherwise the picture will be unnatural, creating disturbing double shadows. On distant scenes, continue to work against the light, using fill-in flash for foreground. The open sky gives much fill-in light and will provide enough distant fill. Scenes with front lighting are usually flat and uninteresting.

Ask your photo dealer to sell you the pocket-size A.R.21 guide, which answers most technical photo queries. It costs $2.00. Also ask for color photography booklets such as Kodak publication E-75.

You will surprise your friends with the superior quality of the pictures and slides you get with sunlight plus flash exposures.

For best results shoot pictures before 10 A.M. and after 2 P.M.

You can even go a step farther in getting better saturation of color in the print or slide. Use a polarizing screen over your lens to avoid the common, flat-lighting effect. This is an inexpensive element that comes in any size you need to screw onto whatever lenses you use.

Pictures should be shot before 10:00 in the morning and after 2:00 in the afternoon to get the best results. Avoid the high noon hours, except in midwinter, at certain latitudes, when the sun hangs low.

Panic in the Night

Living on the wilderness perimeter for months at a time, my door has had its share of knocks by panic in the night. The dark hours shroud the wilderness, drastically changing it for those not accustomeed to its altered, nocturnal complexity. Landmarks are gone on wilderness waters, and only the barely distinguishable outline of the forest treeline against the sky can give a perceptible clue to one's whereabouts.

One night around 11:00 as I lay in bed reading, I heard sounds and voices at the waterfront. It was too late for visitors, and I quickly dressed and prepared for whatever contingency. A middle-aged couple lost on the lake had seen my light over the water from afar and sought help. They had employed a guide a few days earlier, after which they tried on their own to travel by boat and motor through a thirty-five-mile lake, complicated by points, islands, and deep bays. The lady was emotionally exhausted. Since I was occupying a tiny construction shed at the time while building my main cabin, she wanted to know if they could sleep on the floor overnight and seek their rented cabin in the morning.

I heated some water for coffee or tea and set out some food; they had not eaten since their shore lunch at noon.

"You're only a few miles from your cabin," I explained. "Relax for a while and I'll take you to it."

Panic seized them again. The thought of venturing out onto that jet-black lake again after their experience was unthinkable.

I responded with amusement, assuring them that night

travel on the lake had become routine. The trip to their cabin was no navigation problem. When they finally reached the waterfront where their cabin was located, they didn't recognize it and were convinced of their whereabouts only when they found their own belongings in the cabin. The lady feared I'd get lost on the lake while returning to my own cabin. "Ships and planes," I assured her, "cross the ocean while passengers sleep confidently. It's a matter of the simplest orientation for me to return to my cabin, so sleep soundly, and tomorrow, if you care to visit me, we can discuss what you did wrong on your lake venture."

Night draws the curtain for many people, but the strange aspect is that it also dampens their reason and conjures up strange fears.

Perhaps one of the greatest inhibitors to travel in the wilds at any time is the fear of getting lost. It is a legitimate fear for most people. Searching for lost people in the Canadian and Alaskan wilds runs into vast sums for the two governments—Canada and the United States.

Essentially, the problem lies not so much in the failure of wilderness travelers to supply themselves with maps, but in the problem of relating a wilderness area to the map. If you were flying on a clear day at substantial heights, the shape of a water area or a land mass could more readily be identified on the map. But as you travel by canoe, the water areas and land masses have little to identify them with portions of the map. The view of a dozen islands, for example, can look much like a land mass, main shore.

I sought to resolve this problem by publishing a book, *The Wilderness Route Finder*, in direct, nontechnical language. Beside the elementary methods of orienteering, it provides a simple formula for using a sextant to find your latitude, which in itself is a valuable accomplishment in wilderness travel, since a celestially computed latitude line across the shore of a body of water is often a sufficient coordinate (latitude line plus shoreline) to establish one's exact position. Fixing a position by both latitude and longitude without a lakeshore or other line to find a coordinate involves some arithmetic, but the text is simple enough for anyone who has his wits about him.

Sextants for measuring the altitude of the sun or a star have appeared now and then on the government surplus market. Instruments that originally cost $500, are being sold for a small fraction of that. However, they are becoming less and less available as time passes. Used, lightweight field theodolites in good condition serve the same general purpose, but cost considerably more than the government surplus sextants. The Marine-type sextant can be used in conjunction with a separate artificial horizon. A low-cost, plastic sextant is now on the market, which can be used for practice. It is used along with an artificial horizon that's provided.

Protectiveness

We tend to protect our possessions from the bumps and scuffs of living and travel by sheathing them so thoroughly that their utility is handicapped. The protective sheath or case becomes so elegant that we have to protect it, too.

Long ago on wilderness trips I concluded that much of my cased equipment was too inaccessible. I solved the problem by disposing of most of those cases, protecting only those items that stood the greatest risk of being broken. Things got bumped and scuffed a bit, but I liked to say they had a *used* look; they, too, wore the marks of experience.

Perhaps we keep even our thoughts encased too much, and might release our tensions by revealing them. If they get bumped and scuffed in the process of exposure, perhaps they will take on the "used" look of rationality and mellow maturity.

The Speech of Chief Seattle

When it was announced in 1971 that the James Bay hydro-electric project planned to dam or divert all the major rivers of James Bay and build powerhouses on them, it was a sad day indeed.

The area to be destroyed by flooding is unquestionably one of the most spectacularly grand wilderness areas in the world, covering about 133,000 square miles. Where now the tumbling rivers and forest amaze and inspire, there will soon be floodwaters and black, skeletal trunks of dead trees. The floodwaters will rise to great heights and then will be seasonally drained to power turbines. The horrible devastation will remain exposed until the deathlike scene is again covered by water in the annual damming and draining process.

Khrushchev said he would bury us, but perhaps we will beat him to it by drawing a robe of asphalt over ourselves.

Some 6,000 Indians will be driven out by the flooding of their lands—a pittance of consoling cash offered them for the destruction of their ancestral habitat.

The action instituted by the Indians to halt the devastation has the familiar ring that we have heard down through history—a semblance of judicial deliberation with an always predictable verdict against the Indian.

That the project will flood the Indian burial grounds and destroy the Indians' way of life is no more regretted now than were similar actions in the past.

Perhaps the most absurd arguments presented in the hearings is that since the Indian has availed himself of the white man's manufactured goods in exchange for trapped furs, therefore the Indian has resigned himself to the white man's ways and should be absorbed in the white man's industrial obsession. How obtuse!

When an executive of a large insurance company told his sales force that he wants salesmen who think, feel, eat, play, dream, and live insurance, we get some idea of the great mistake that can be made if cultural values and life standards are left in the hands of industry and business.

The James Bay project has been fully documented, is available to the reader, and needs no detailing here. The malpractice in the treatment of the Indian has been going on for a long time and is best depicted in the speech of Chief Seattle, given well over a century ago.

Few world leaders have assured their reputations for the ages with great and prophetic sayings. But Chief Seattle uttered a profound truth, one we need to ponder, in his famous 1854 speech during the transfer of ancestral lands to the Federal Government, "The earth does not belong to man; man belongs to the earth." The speech was translated by William Arrowsmith. The emergence of the Indian today, demanding his rights, makes the speech unusually significant and timely; it should be read by every living human being. It typifies what is going on in the James Bay project:

The Great Chief in Washington sends word that he wishes to buy our land.

The Great Chief also sends us words of friendship and good will. This is kind of him, since we know he has little need of our friendship in return. But we will consider your offer. For we know that if we do not sell, the white man may come with guns and take our land.

How can you buy or sell the sky, the warmth of the land? The idea is strange to us.

If we do not own the freshness of the air and the sparkle of the water, how can you buy them?

Every part of this earth is sacred to my people. Every shining pine needle, every sandy shore, every mist in the dark woods, every clearing, and humming insect is holy in the memory and experience of my people. The sap which courses through the trees carries the memories of the red man.

The white man's dead forget the country of their birth when they go to walk among the stars. Our dead never forget this beautiful earth, for it is the mother of the red man. We are part of the earth and it is part of us. The perfumed flowers are our sisters; the deer, the horse, the juices in the meadows, the body heat of the pony, and man—all belong to the same family.

So, when the Great Chief in Washington sends word that he wishes to buy our land, he asks much of us.

The Great Chief sends word he will reserve us a place so that we can live comfortably to ourselves. He will be our father and we will be his children.

So we will consider your offer to buy our land. But it will not be easy. For this land is sacred to us.

This shining water that moves in the streams and rivers is not just water but the blood of our ancestors. If we sell you land, you must remember that it is sacred, and you must teach your children that it is sacred, and that each ghostly reflection in the clear water of the lakes tells of events and memories in the life of my people. The water's murmur is the voice of the father's father.

The rivers are our brothers, they quench our thirst. The rivers carry our canoes, and feed our children. If we sell you our land, you must remember, and teach your children, that the rivers are our brothers, and yours, and you must henceforth give the rivers the kindness you would give any brother.

The red man has always retreated before the advancing white man, as the mist of the mountain runs before the morning sun. But the ashes of our fathers are sacred. Their graves are holy ground, and so these hills, these trees, this portion of the earth is consecrated to us. We know that the white man does not understand our ways. One portion of land is the same to him as the next, for he is a stranger who comes in the night and takes from the land whatever he needs. The earth is not his brother, but his enemy, and when he has conquered it, he moves on. He leaves his father's graves behind, and he does not care. He kidnaps the earth from his children. He does not care. His father's graves and his children's birthright are forgotten. He treats his mother, the earth, and his brother, the sky, as things to be bought, plundered, sold like sheep or bright beads. His appetite will devour the earth and leave behind only a desert.

I do not know. Our ways are different from your ways. The sight of your cities pains the eyes of the red man. But perhaps it is because the red man is a savage and does not understand.

There is no quiet place in the white man's cities. No place to hear the unfurling of leaves in spring or the rustle of insect's wings. But perhaps it is because I am a savage and do not understand. The clatter only seems to insult the ears. And what is there to life if a man cannot hear the lonely cry of the whippoorwill or the arguments of the frogs around a pond at night? I am a red man and do not understand. The Indian prefers the soft sound of the wind darting over the face of a pond, and the smell of the wind itself, cleansed by a midday rain, or scented with the piñon pine.

The air is precious to the red man, for all things share the same breath—the beast, the tree, the man, they all share the same breath. The white man does not seem to notice the air he breathes. Like a man dying for many days, he is numb to the stench. But if we sell you our land, you must remember that the air is precious to us, that the air shares its spirit with all the life it supports. The wind that gave our grandfather his first breath also receives his last sight. And the wind must also give our children the spirit of life. And if we sell you our land, you must keep it apart and sacred, as a place where even the white man can go to taste the wind that is sweetened by the meadow's flowers.

So we will consider your offer to buy our land. If we decide to accept, I will make one condition: The white man must treat the beasts of this land as his brothers.

I am a savage and I do not understand any other way. I have seen a thousand rotting buffalos on the prairie, left by the white man who shot them from a passing train. I am a savage and I do not understand how the smoking iron horse can be more important than the buffalo that we kill only to stay alive.

What is man without the beasts? If all the beasts were gone, men would die from a great loneliness of spirit. For whatever happens to the beasts, soon happens to man. All things are connected.

You must teach your children that the ground beneath their feet is the ashes of our grandfathers. So that they will respect the land, tell your children that the earth is rich with the lives of our kin. Teach your children what we have taught our children, that the earth is our mother. Whatever befalls the earth, befalls the sons of the earth. If men spit upon the ground, they spit upon themselves.

This we know. The earth does not belong to man; man belongs to the earth. This we know. All things are connected like the blood which unites one family. All things are connected.

Whatever befalls the earth befalls the sons of the earth. Man did not weave the web of life; he is merely a strand in it. Whatever he does to the web, he does to himself.

But we will consider your offer to go to the reservation you have for my people. We will live apart, and in peace. It matters little where we spend the rest of our days. Our children have seen their fathers humbled in defeat. Our warriors have felt shame, and after defeat they turn their days in idleness and contaminate their bodies with sweet foods and strong drink. It matters little where we pass the rest of our days. They are not many. A few more hours, a few more winters, and none of the children of the great tribes that once lived on this earth or that

134

roam now in small bands in the woods will be left to mourn the graves of a people once as powerful and hopeful as yours. But why should I mourn the passing of my people? Tribes are made of men, nothing more. Men come and go, like the waves of the sea.

Even the white man, whose God walks and talks with him as friend to friend, cannot be exempt from the common destiny. We may be brothers after all; we shall see. One thing we know, which the white man may one day discover—our God is the same God. You may think now that you own Him as you wish to own our land; but you cannot. He is the God of man, and His compassion is equal for the red man and the white. This earth is precious to Him, and to harm the earth is to heap contempt on its Creator. The whites too shall pass; perhaps sooner than all other tribes. Continue to contaminate your bed, and you will one night suffocate in your own waste.

But in your perishing you will shine brightly, fired by the strength of the God who brought you to this land and for some special purpose gave you dominion over this land and over the red man. That destiny is a mystery to us, for we do not understand when the buffalo are all slaughtered, the wild horses are tamed, the secret corners of the forest heavy with the scent of many men, and the view of the ripe hills blotted by talking wires. Where is the thicket? Gone. Where is the eagle? Gone. And what is it to say good-bye to the swift pony and the hunt? The end of living and the beginning of survival.

So we will consider your offer to buy our land. If we agree, it will be to secure the reservation you have promised. There, perhaps, we may live out our brief days as we wish. When the last red man has vanished from this earth, and his memory is only the shadow of a cloud moving across the prairie, these shores and forests will still hold the spirits of my people. For they love this earth as the newborn loves its mother's heartbeat. So if we sell you our land, love it as we've loved it. Care for it as we've cared for it. Hold in your mind the memory of the land as it is when you take it. And with all your strength, with all your mind, with all your heart, preserve it for your children, and love it . . . as God loves us all.

One thing we know. Our God is the same God. This earth is precious to him. Even the white man cannot be exempt from the common destiny. We may be brothers after all. We shall see.

On Flexing One's Legs

When I've hiked the half-mile along the road from my home to the village general store or the post office, I've often been offered a ride—the donor seeming to pity me. This has become less frequent of late because I have been inviting the drivers to park their cars beside the road and walk with me. When they learn that parked at my residence is a practically new car, and still I walk, carrying my purchases in a pack, they can't understand why I need to hike.

On Happiness

I was happy in those youthful days even when austerity arose with me each morning. As a boy seeking the wilderness I had no money for camping gear, and so I slept with a blanket of dry leaves heaped on me for warmth. While I also went to bed with austerity, I nevertheless slept well, and rose happily with the dawn. When I gained some affluence I did not greatly increase my happiness, and I am inclined to think that if I lost what money and possessions I now have, I would still be happy, because I would always have the inexhaustible treasure of wilderness to fall back on.

The secret, I think, lies in the fact that most of the artifacts of civilization eventually wind up obsolete on the junk heap. The eternal wilderness, however, refreshes and recycles itself.

I had a commitment to happiness.

Preservation by Natural Means

Perhaps the most refreshing change in our understanding is that we have at last recognized the hazards of breaking ecological chains. Lately, we have begun to defer to natural methods to preserve wildlife and maintain a balanced agriculture.

The subject is broad; you can investigate it at length in government agriculture bulletins, but an example or two may point the way.

The population of skunks and ducks may seem to be unrelated. Yet, they are interdependent. Skunks eat many turtle eggs which they dig out of the sand. Often considered a nuisance, many skunks have been destroyed. The turtles then multiplied prolifically, hazarding the duck population. Young ducks were destroyed in vast numbers when turtles, coming up from below, grabbed the young ducks by their legs, and pulled them underwater.

Ladybugs prey on aphids and other small insects. Their value has proven so great that ladybugs can now be purchased in quantity commercially. You may wonder how so many ladybugs can be found. Early in September they congregate in massive numbers as they move in toward their wintering-over sites. On cold and overcast days, millions are discovered inches deep under fallen leaves.

Thus we are very gradually finding the safest and most logical ways to keep the ecological process going as nature has done for millions of years in a balance which man, heretofore, has failed to accomplish or fully understand.

There must have been natural countervailing forces acting through millenia; otherwise the world would have been overrun by several species. Man may be one of those. Our job is to find and use the appropriate countervailing natural forces whenever a portion of the ecological scheme needs to be rebalanced. Our science is not yet adequate to the task but we can't delay long. The poisonous insecticides we spread work incalculable and long lasting damage to the ecology.

Wilderness Fantasy

In no department of human experience, it seems, has there been more fiction, fancy, supernaturalism, and illusion, than in the popular concept and depiction of wilderness.

The compelling urge felt by a large number of writers and artists to distort it suggests that they fail to grasp its real magnificence and profound values. We, of course, have to presume that the effect of wilderness on each of us can be quite different. But why it should be treated as absurd fantasy, escapes me. Nature overwhelms in its reality.

Some fiction writers have timber wolves surrounding a camp, the campers throwing glowing fagots to stay the wolves' encroachment. Others have weasels leaping from trees to the throats of woodsmen, bent on sucking the victims' blood. Others have ghost images lurking back in the shadows, uttering sounds that are purported to resemble neither forest creatures nor human beings. The wind

The commonly misunderstood timber wolf (COURTESY OF BARBARA VON HOFFMAN)

howls ill omens of impending, unavoidable doom, and the thundering waterfall houses monsters beneath its cataract. In waters lurks the Loch Ness monster and in the mountains the Abominable Snowman, and "Bigfoot," half man and half beast—all figments of the most senseless credulity.

A vast population evidently fear wilderness in any form, so this reaction to it should not seem strange. It is not very flattering to my experience, with about half of my time lived in the wilds, that in eighty years I have not seen, heard, or been stalked by any of the current bogies. I have found the wilderness, in spite of its rigors at times, a comforting, peaceful, generous environment.

We should be more trusting, more abiding, more respectful, less timorous; and at least be rational so that our associations with nature will be wondrous and enjoyable rather than illusory, noxious, and stupid.

". . . I have found the wilderness . . . a comforting, peaceful, generous environment."

". . . our association with Nature will be wondrous . . ."

The Human Coral Reef

Down through the years we have seen much emphasis placed on family succession in business and industry—symbolically the coral reef, calcareous creatures building upon calcareous creatures, son following father, generation after generation.

Sometimes, happily of late, the traditional successions appear to be breaking up; what was rare wine for the father, seems to be small beer for the son. Here in the following may be an example:

My Indian canoe partner and I were entering an Ontario wilderness lake from a portage when about noon we observed two men on an island a half mile or so down the lake. We concluded from the size of the small fire that they were having their lunch. Since we were deep in the wilds and hadn't seen anyone for over two weeks, 5e were naturally curious about who they were. We paddled toward the island, hoping that as we passed we might get an amicable nod to open a conversation. We got more—an invitation to lunch.

One of the two men was an Indian; the other proved to be a member of a nationally-known, aristocratic family, whom I must leave unnamed. My Indian partner and the Indian on the island were acquainted some years back, which helped congenially for all, even though they talked to each other largely in Cree. This drew them together while the white member and I found a bedrock ledge at the water's edge where we sat and visited at considerable length.

When he introduced himself his name sounded familiar, and I jested about it. He made no immediate reply. As the conversation drew on I became aware from his inferences that he was in fact a member of that famous family.

Middle-aged and with business responsibilities, it seemed strange that he would be spending the rather protracted period of several months in the wilds, while the responsibility was delegated to others. He seemed willing enough to discuss his viewpoint but was a bit apprehensive that I, as a writer, might make hay of it as a news story. "I'm on your side," I assured him. "Why should I betray a confidence?"

I referred to the symbolism of the coral reef, but only after he had preceded it with a similar analogy.

"Think of all the jewelry that could be made from the coral in the piled-up reef and island," I said facetiously.

"That's it," he replied. "Wealth. I don't want to give the best of my life to produce a mass of dead, calcareous material, no matter how valuable."

"Money, you mean," I added.

"Yes, money," was his reply.

We pitched our camps together on the island, talking far into the night before a campfire, about life in general, about its values and briefness, how one should use the limited time one has. The next morning, as we went our separate ways in canoes, I told him, "If you're at all interested in my business appraisal, I think that when you traded your briefcase for a packsack, it was your most successful and noble transaction."

Mutability

Anxious survivors of soldiers missing in action naturally demand that strenuous efforts be made to find them.

We need to remember that soon after a human or an animal dies in the wilds, left undiscovered, the body deteriorates rapidly. The human body is mostly water, and it soon virtually "evaporates" into the air to be blown over land and sea. There's little left and that residue soon blends naturally into the earth's accumulating humus and disappears.

Is it not the most ideal and beautiful way to return to the earth from which we came? Indians for many centuries raised their dead on pole scaffolds, so that their bodies would, by exposure, gradually return to the elements. "I am," they proclaim, "the essence of what the earth is."

Is it not fitting that the molecular body be returned to the molecular earth? To know that we become the atomic component of a subsequent tree that rises, a flower that blooms, an eagle that soars, the "voice of the rapids," or the surging sea, possibly of another human being, is to blend in perpetuity with the vibrant earth. I like to believe that my body may be partly composed of the chemistry of a feather that fell from a bird in flight a thousand years ago, from a shaft of lightning, a sunbeam, an arrow that fell when primordial man roamed the earth.

The winds of the earth, the sun and rain, thus, move the elements of our integrating bodies, to become "the essence of what the earth is."

Survivors—can we not be satisfied with this magnificence

An eagle in flight

in Nature's scheme? Is the essence not as great as the physical form?

> Leaf after leaf drops off, flower
> after flower,
> Some in the chill, some in the
> warmer hour:
> Alive they flourish, and alive
> they fall,
> And Earth who nourished them
> receives them all.
> Should we, her wiser sons, be
> less content
> To sink into her lap when life is
> spent?
> "Leaf After Leaf Drops Off."
> Walter Savage Landor

The Seasonal Miracle

Sunday, the first weekend in October, there are great traffic jams in the northern United States and southern Canadian provinces. Is it a national and international event that causes it? Yes, the autumn coloring reaches its peak.

When people will move out in their cars into the outlying country, bumper to bumper to observe the magnificence of Nature, I have no fear that we will wholly lose our natural resources to encroaching ravage.

A Sexual Complex

It was our first camp on the Big Fork River in the fall of 1914, the beginning of a three and one-half months' canoe journey. We were two eighteen-year olds, charmed by the wilderness which then, in that region of northern Minnesota, was inviolate.

The river flowed north to the Canadian boundary, emptying into the Rainy River, which connects Lake of the Woods and Rainy Lake.

In our young minds we were undaunted adventurers. We had heard about the Muldoon Rapids on our route downriver where a team of horses and a wagon had been swept away on a ford, killing the horses and crushing the wagon. We were told about other whitewater and Grand Falls—which, in the prospect of adventure, we were eager to reach.

We had never seen a native woods Indian, so that when two came by our camp in a birchbark canoe and buckskin shirts, the magic of the wilderness was intensified beyond anything we had expected. We asked them to stop for a cup of tea. They were headed for the settlement of Big Fork, Minnesota, to pick up supplies.

When they left our camp, we handed them two penny postcards to mail, addressed to our parents, on which we had written that the cards would be mailed by Indians. This, we felt, gave the cards great significance. As they left, they asked if there was anything else we wanted them to bring back, since they would be on our same route on their return. Meant merely as a youthful wisecrack, I said, "Yes, if you want to send down a couple of pretty girls." They smiled and went on.

The author at age eighteen

Several days later at one of our camps, a canoe pulled up in which were two attractive young Indian girls, explaining that we had asked for them. We were both amused and frightened. How do you handle a situation like this? They had brought along rabbit-skin sleeping robes and an extra tent.

It was mealtime, so we prepared to show them at least the hospitality of a meal. No sooner had we begun to gather a little wood for a tea fire when they elbowed us out of the way and took over.

Needless to say, the situation was getting more difficult by the minute. Men caught under the mandate of feminine influence become poltroons.

Just how we managed the situation I do not recall in detail, but it must have been akin to the sailor's unkept promise that when the ship again returned to port the good life would be resumed. We didn't tell them that our request for girls had been merely a joke. Perhaps to the two male Indians it was good follow-up humor.

About a week later we came upon a cabin and small homestead clearing at the junction of Deer Creek and the Big Fork River. The resident was a trapper and bush farmer, a rather brusque man but, as we learned, a kindly man. He apparently liked our company, since he urged us to stay on for a while in our camp, and provided us with fresh vegetables and venison. Before the day was over, we concluded that where the wilderness was concerned, he had the wisdom of the ages. We learned much—actually a valuable briefing that held through our whole journey, and memorably since.

Just before leaving we told him about the embarrassing situation we had created with the Indian girls, "What would you have done in a situation like that?" I asked.

He didn't hesitate for a moment. "I would do just what you did, only I wouldn't lie about it."

"In wildness is the preservation of the world."

Postmortem

H. L. Mencken said that if you want to do something for him after he is gone, "Smile at a homely girl."

I have a request. If you want to do something for me after I am gone, live so as not to defile the precious earth.

The Omnipresence of Nature

When I meet a friend, acquaintance, or prominent person I've not seen for some time, I note that he's aged, and am reminded that Nature keeps a time schedule on all of us. But there's a kind of consolation in knowing that wealth and fame are not compensating factors in Nature's computation of time.

"Nature is keeping a time schedule on all of us."

I tell people—too advisedly, perhaps—that the aging process might become a little slower if they were exposed more to a natural environment and less to the urban grind. Most, though, continue to sacrifice their health and well-being on the altars of Mammon. Thoreau said, "They will find that it is a fool's life before they get to the end of it." When he dallied through the day, or in sitting in the sun contemplating Nature for hours, he found, "They were not time subtracted from my life, but so much over my usual allowance."

From the City to the Wilderness

When I speak about abandoning life in a metropolis for a more natural existence, I am not recommending that you move abruptly from the intensity of the urban environment to the remote wilds. There should be a transition process. You'll want to consider moving to nearby suburbia or outer suburbia; some few to the wilderness fringe. In the rare and special case only, will it be to the remote interior wilderness.

Each individual will, of course, discover the degree of remoteness he needs. I can only tell you what I have seen the situation to be among those making the move.

The arterial highway makes access to suburbia or even outer suburbia a simple matter to commute to your job. City people often find that first move easier to adjust to if their new home is in a small residential cluster, rather than

152

isolated even by a mile or two from a neighbor. Too sudden and complete a divorce from accustomed amenities may have you feeling like a "fish out of water."

Those who are thinking about plunging right into the interior of the wilds might better consider trying life on the wilderness perimeter first. Most who go all the way at the beginning almost inevitably later move back to the perimeter. The avid wilderness sentimentalist endeavoring to escape from the trials and tribulations of humanity usually has a process of modification to undergo before he finds his best niche. It will usually be that kind of life on the perimeter where he can place one hand on the wilds, the other on the humanity from which he thought to escape.

Even then, unless he has a strong individualism, he may find himself the regretful expatriate, cut off at least in part from his needs. There can be a sudden feeling of ostracism where life had long been through habit, caught up by the crowd spirit.

Deurbanization isn't achieved easily. Those used to taking the cues for their life from city culture will find sudden freedom a shock. The aspiring individualist with few inner resources may be bitterly disappointed.

For a writer or painter, the move can be found invaluable. Where in the city it was difficult to glean even a few hours from outside social bombardment, interrupting serious work, he now has both room and time to flex his spiritual muscles. Others less endowed with those faculties need to set a more utilitarian course. It takes time to accommodate the reflexes, reactions of a lifetime. But the tension of memory can be adjusted when you pick up new interests. Blessed solitude and individual achievement are the rewards that make the effort worthwhile.

The Wilderness Cache

History recounts great dramas of exploration parties saving themselves by fighting their way back to supply caches. Today's mechanical means of travel make caches less necessary. Yet trappers and those using the more elementary methods of travel still fall back on the traditional cache.

The security of the cache has never been easy to maintain. The open swamp was occasionally the location of a cache when the hazard of forest fire was a possibility. Though reasonably safe from fire there, its owners found it difficult to reach. A tower had to be built with supports which could not be scaled by bears or wolverines. The perfect cache was never achieved and, too often, because of this, tragedy struck many an expedition.

In earlier days I risked the lesser hazard of forest fire against the greater hazard of disturbance by wildlife, stretching a stranded wire cable between upland trees and hanging the cache midway on the cable in a can which originally had contained fifty pounds of commercial lard.

Other times I'd hang the cache on branches thrust from a fairly high bank over the water of a river. The branches had to be thin and flexible enough to prevent their supporting heavy animals.

The elevated tower cache shown in the illustration has been the standard structure for centuries. The cache is approached with a ladder, the ladder removed to keep bears, wolverines, and other creatures from the food. Note also the baffle at the base of the upper structure. The main upper structure would be vulnerable if it was on the

"The elevated tower cache . . . the standard structure for centuries" (COURTESY OF RAY TREMBLAY)

ground level. The raised cache is secure if the creature can be kept off the roof, and the baffle serves that purpose. Tin roofs are best for cache buildings on the ground, since they're impervious to bear or wolverine claws.

Rescue

It was in the early 1920s. My partner and I had crowded the open-water season well into late fall, breaking some thin ice on the last lap of an almost-two-months' canoe trip in Ontario and Manitoba. When we completed the trip, we drove down from Canada in a Model T Ford, arriving in Grand Marais, Minnesota on the shore of Lake Superior, in time for supper at the East Bay Hotel.

The sky was building up for a snowstorm. We expected it to start before nightfall, but it held off until early morning. Arising early, we decided to make a run for it to Duluth, through the heavily falling snow. Several concerned people warned that we might get stuck long before we reached Duluth. We risked it—and lost.

Far along on the highway, as the snow deepened, the Model T radiator began to steam, despite the numerous snowballs we had dropped into its radiator. We had wound some heavy hemp ropes around the tires, running the rope between the wood spokes—the wheel construction at that time. It helped the traction, but finally the snow became too deep to continue in high gear, and there was no middle gear in a Model T. We managed to get the steaming car off the road center, which by now was difficult to determine in the drifts.

It had become obvious to the authorities and people back in Grand Marais, who knew of our departure, that we couldn't have reached Two Harbors or Duluth. The snow had gotten too deep too quickly.

There were growing apprehensions among fine, weather-experienced citizens of Grand Marais that we might be found frozen to death in our stalled Model T. The authorities deemed it necessary, therefore, to get out their heaviest snow plow to reach us, even before the storm had abated. When the plow reached the car, it was identified only by a mound of drifted snow. The two men on the plow shoveled away enough snow to get a door open, and found the car empty.

The wind was not wholly favorable to detect our campfire, but whirling and buffeting against the forest, a faint fragrance of woodsmoke did reach them. The howling wind and driving snow greatly muffled their voices as they called out loudly. We answered, giving them the direction to reach us in a dense, protective grove of conifers.

I met them as they came on snowshoes. "Are you okay?" they asked apprehensively.

"We're perfectly okay," I said. "You're just in time for some hot coffee and coffee-cake bannock."

At our cozy camp before a large open fire they sat upon rolled-up, down sleeping bags, drinking hot coffee, looking out into the lee opening of a lean-to, made with poles and balsam boughs, the wedge tent flattened as a tarp roof covering on the lean-to. The wind continued to howl and create enormous drifts. Our car was by now merely another undulation of the deep, drifting snow.

They asked if we wanted to follow the plow back to Grand Marais, but we respectfully and gratefully declined, since we were comfortably camped. Two days later, we pulled camp, dug the Model T out of its snowy depths, and continued on to Duluth in the wake of a scheduled snowplow routinely servicing the road from the east.

"Rescue" was complete.

"At our cozy camp before a large open fire . . ."

The Calculated Risk

An old Indian proverb says that only the foolhardy run
rapids that are too hazardous; that's why, as a result, there

"I now portage around certain rapids I once intrepidly ran . . ."

are fewer fools in the world than there might otherwise be. The difference between a foolhardy individual and a courageous one is that the latter has a better faculty for determining what might be the safest calculated risk.

I now portage around certain rapids I once intrepidly ran with a canoe. This has become less a matter of timidity than of having learned in later years by experience what is foolhardy and what is not.

There are many graves which might be marked with the epitaph:

I WAS INTREPID

Women's Lib

Here at our wilderness cabin in Canada's wilds at this writing, it has occurred to my wife and me that Women's Lib in its best sense reached the two of us long, long ago.

This morning I worked with chain saw, block-and-tackle, and other gear to put in more firewood. It was as natural and presumed that my wife should be a part of this operation as it was for me to make dinner last evening when she was involved in hemming up some needed curtains.

It has been said that two people working together as a team can accomplish as much as three people each working separately. In the building of our own cabins through the years, my wife became indispensable in holding up the other end of any item needing two-person support while it got nailed into position. She feeds the sticks of firewood along the sawbuck while I lop off the lengths to proper burning size with a chain saw. She won't let me wash dishes because I never seem to get things put back where she can find them again, which has increased my pleasure,

"It was ... natural ... that my wife should be a part of this operation ..."

of course. But I get in on a number of domestic tasks that relieve her of doing them when she becomes involved in others ordinarily attributed to my lot.

Priceless Possessions

Strange is the value placed on material possessions. Those items which we can readily afford to replace shrink in value.

I would trade a dozen canoe paddles even-up for three of the same quality and dimension if I had to bother storing the extra nine. The three I use are periodically sanded, oiled, and hand-rubbed until their feel and balance become so familiar that I could recognize them in the dark.

Among my most cherished possessions I have a canvas bag of rawhide strips, Indian-tanned moosehides, square flipper seal hides for soles, and incidental equipment for fabricating special items that cannot be found in the market.

Why should I dote on such trivia? Perhaps it's just because the contents of my "bag of tricks" can't be purchased in stores. The rawhide; moosehides from which I make my own unique patterns of moccasins and mittens; the seal hide I got from the Eskimos for mukluk soles; the compound I put on my tent ropes to preserve them against weather, against gnawing rodents, and to give them both strength and better tying quality; the cruiser ax that I ground to efficient chopping thinness and to which I replaced a better balanced, truer, hickory handle—these and a number of other self-crafted items I prize more than expensive commercial substitutes.

I once bought some attractive compact field glasses in a store. The lenses are excellent, but after some use the paper-thin leather veneer over an understiffening of card-board was scuffed through, and the dishonor of the casemaker revealed. I wondered, did the optical firm do an honest job on the glasses only to contract with a dishonest leather goods firm for the case? I subsequently sent the shoddy case back to the optical company, and asked them to supply a serviceable case. They responded honestly, to my surprise, by canceling all future distribution of such shoddy products. Perhaps there is some decency around if we'll take the trouble to search it out.

The Insignificant Tiny Seed

In youth we see the tiny seed and announce in half-belief that from that seed will grow a giant tree. In youth there is a kind of immortality of self, a vague time equation existing between the seed and the potential giant tree. I've recently passed my eighty-second birthday, and can now exclaim with George Bernard Shaw, "Oh, to be eighty again!" Now I can equate with the full-grown tree that came from the tiny seed, although in youth I would not have believed it would happen so soon.

About sixty years ago I received a small packet of white pine and red pine seeds from a seed nursery in Pennsylvania. I planted them here and there on the five-acre tract on the St. Croix River, where my wife and I now have our outer-suburban home. I thought it quite an accomplishment that with the planting and watering they became little seedlings in a few years, and at that point I felt them coeval with my youth.

Coeval with my advanced years, they now tower into the air where my arms will not reach around them.

The long interval between seed and giant tree? It seems but a fleeting moment. "A human life" in the infinity of time, someone said, is but a "star gleam on a stone." Perhaps a little longer than that, but we should treasure every moment.

Wilderness Bread

When man first discovered that he could stone-grind various seeds and invent flour to make bread, he probably baked it first by wrapping dough around a stick and baking it near the flame by reflection. Many peoples do it that way even today.

Perhaps the next method of baking was to heat flat rocks and use a combination of rock-retained heat and reflection. It is likely that the Horno or beehive oven might have followed.

With today's metal utensils, there are three wilderness methods of baking: in packhorse country, the Dutch oven is most popular; in canoe country, the reflector oven; and while backpacking, the bannock method, using a fry pan. In recent years I have gone solely to the bannock method on all types of wilderness travel. It's simple, and needs no other equipment than a utility fry pan. It produces that tasty brown-crust loaf with the least effort. Since it requires an active flame, bannock is usually baked in the evening while the camper sits at his comfort fire. For complete information on wilderness baking and cooking methods, see my book *The New Way of the Wilderness*, available in both paperback and hardcover editions.

The Dutch oven

The reflector oven

End product from the reflector oven (Early photo of the author.)

The bannock or fry pan supported before an open fire

Wilderness Companionship

One of my readers wrote to ask if I would tell him the qualities to look for in a companion for an extensive canoe trip, and how to maintain the best possible relationship.

I can't think of a simple answer. A hippie hitchhiker once told his driver host, a man who troubled himself about a lot of trivia, "Don't fret the small stuff." The major undertakings and challenges on a canoe voyage, or other kind of wilderness trip, do not as a rule cause the vexations which lead to friction. It's the "small stuff," the daily aggravations, difference in opinion on camp and travel methods, orientation problems, choice of food, and so on, at times, nothing apparent that causes stress. The slight, chronic bumping of a paddle against the canoe, for example, or some other such petty annoyance, may be impossible to stop without offense, and may grow into a serious breach.

To depend on friendships alone to bridge gaps of daily aggravation can be a mistake. I like the revealing story of the Missouri mule driver who said that those animals are very much like friends—they will respond to your wishes for twenty years just for the opportunity to give you one devastating kick.

I rescued a bee that found its way into my cabin. It was feeble from its long beating against the windowpane to get out, so I placed some honey in water and let the bee drink some of it. As its strength came back, I took it outdoors on a sheet of paper under an inverted water glass. I tossed the bee into the air for a takeoff. It came back, stung me, then flew away.

". . . to know the qualities to look for in a companion on an extensive canoe trip."

Summer Heat and Insects

Summer heat and insects were a common problem in my wilderness life until I discovered that close to and on the proper side of such cold bodies of water as Lake Superior and Great Bear Lake neither heat nor insects are a problem. But then the tent or the cabin must be fairly close to the waterfront. Islands in such lakes have great midsummer camping advantages; however, one must take special care in canoe and boat travel to and from them, since rough seas and even dense fog can create risks on such large lakes.

Some of these lines are being written in mid-July on Canada's cool and bugless Lake Superior North Shore, fifteen miles from the famous Grand Portage, while much of the country is sweltering in 90° heat.

Change of latitude does not always bring a change of temperature. Thousands drive north in midsummer to reach cool climates, only to find that sunlit days are much longer than in the South and the heat is often just as oppressive. I once experienced a temperature of over 100° north of the Arctic Circle. In the land of the midnight sun, there are few night, earth-cooling hours.

In mountainous areas of the Southwest a 1,000-foot change of altitude is supposed to be comparable to 300 miles of latitude. Go high enough and you can even find the equivalent of arctic and alpine tundra, affecting vegetation, animal life, and weather. But the equation isn't a strict one, failing sometimes due to the direction of mountain slopes and other geographical influences.

The cool and bugless Lake Superior shore

The Princess and the Pea

Before the advent of the air mattress we used balsam boughs under our sleeping bags to cushion the hard ground. I awoke one night wondering about the commotion my canoe partner was causing—awake and thrashing around on his side of the tent. Presently, I heard a boulder roll down the bedrock slope in front of our tent and splash into the lake. When my partner had settled back into his sleeping position again, I asked, "What happened?"

"Oh, nothing," he replied, already half-asleep, "I was lying on a folded leaf."

Visitors and Visiting

The expression "dropping in" on one's friends must have started many years ago before planes came into use in the wilds. Where earlier it was used figuratively, it is now at our wilderness cabin used literally. Our cabin, twenty-five miles from an auto road, can readily be reached by pontoon plane. When a plane roars just above our rooftop and then circles for a water landing, we're pretty sure that we are being signaled and that someone is "dropping in."

Friendly bush pilots "drop in" with supplies.

But not always.

Bush planes en route to the Hudson's Bay Company Post at Fort Hope need but a slight detour to pass over our cabin. Friendly pilots with mail or a message buzz our cabin at low level and circle just above the tree tops until we step out on the waterfront in full view. Then they drop our mail packet, contained in a waterproof plastic bag, into the lake.

We push off in a canoe to make the pickup. If we manage to get out on the water before the drop, the pilot often tries to drop the mail packet from the plane into the canoe. We've amusingly offered a rather generous award for anyone who succeeds. No one has yet been able to collect it. We kid the pilots about the accuracy of their "pinpoint" bombing.

Now and then pilots land on the water with provisions or heavy parcel post, or just for a cup of coffee. They taxi to our shore.

Our Indian friends, who come annually by canoe to the North River wild-rice beds, visit us. They have an aversion to just dropping in, believing, they say, that they will interrupt my writing. When they reach a point within hailing distance from our shore they rest on their paddles and modestly wait for an invitation to land, a mere formality, of course.

Living in a remote place allows us to really appreciate some of the little gifts visitors sometimes bring: very perishable, luxurious food items for example. One brought a four-layer cake that was to have the complement of a real whipped cream topping. Rather than risk messing up so fragile a frosting en route, the whipping cream came separate in a carton. And to be sure that it got whipped, a manually operated egg beater was brought.

Two blueberry pies of such thickness and excellence that we were sure they were homemade proved to have been purchased at a supermarket. The label on the pies showed that they were made not in our greatest blueberry country, but in Los Angeles. We later learned that the blueberries had come from the north, been processed in Chicago, made into pies in Los Angeles, and jobbed in another area, finally getting back to the blueberry country. Is this economy?

People who visit us almost invariably stay overnight, due to the cost of getting to us by plane. But we found that distance is pretty much a relative factor. A friend of ours who flies his own twin-motored plane left from an airfield near Minneapolis, landed on an air strip at Sioux Lookout,

"Our Indian friends . . . come annually by canoe to the wild rice beds . . ."

Ontario, then chartered a pontoon plane to reach us. He stayed only for lunch and a two-hour visit, arriving back at his home near Minneapolis the same day. He didn't consider the trip anything extraordinary. It was his usual way of seeing people and carrying on his affairs. I commented on the cost. Like the yacht owner he said, "If you have to ask what it costs, you can't afford it."

Knots

Every human being on earth needs to learn how to tie some knots. We need to know how to handle a rope or cord in simple, everyday life at home, in industry, and camping. Certain knots have special functions; and by daily practice and instruction we can tie them almost by reflex.

Yet, how many people know how to handle a simple piece of cord or rope—advantageously, that is?

My neighbor was cutting down a tree, and he needed to have it fall into an open area. He was using block and tackle (pulleys and rope), and I volunteered to help. As he was about to make a tie on the tree, I said, "Use a bowline." He'd never heard of it. It's a knot that can be given any amount of strain on the pull rope, without the knot becoming tight and difficult to untie. Have you seen people struggling to untie a knot, even using their teeth to undo it?

Tying knots can be an enjoyable pastime; but I don't

like to learn a large number of them, since they are too soon forgotten if not used. We might better learn to tie useful knots—those applicable to our immediate needs. The saying, "Use it or lose it," certainly applies to knots.

Those who live and travel in the wilds should at least be able to tie a bowline, taut-line hitch, timber hitch, half hitch, and whatever other knots apply to their tasks; such as sailing and horse-packing. Most are illustrated in numerous books on knot tying and needn't be repeated here.

One of the most useful knots in packing a sledge in winter wilderness travel, or where tension must be given a rope, is what is most commonly known as the trucker's hitch. It multiplies the tension on a rope by much the same principle as a block and tackle but by using a rope only. Eskimos need to pull heavy animals such as walrus from the water by stringing sealskin "ropes" through ice blocks, using them in place of pulleys. It's the same principle as the trucker's hitch.

When my neighbor left his cabin at the end of the open-water season, he said with a parting smile, "When I see you in the spring, I promise you I'll be able to tie the bowline."

High and Low Sensibility

Over many years of wilderness activity I have discovered two widely divergent kinds of individuals who, for want of better classification, I must refer to as having either a low or a high sensibility.

I knew a cowhand in my own early days in Montana where I did that work, too. This fellow would insert the barrel of his Colt .45 into a loop of barbedwire and use it to twist-tighten a strand while nailing it to a fence post. (The revolver, by the way, was used in those days only to kill a critter hopelessly hung up in a barbedwire fence, or to shoot a horse if a rider was thrown, caught in a stirrup, and being dragged.) I babied my Colt .45, proud that I was quite a fair shot with it. "Fast draw" nonsense never had any appeal for me. I cleaned and oiled my revolver regularly. My comrade, however, never cleaned his, nor was he interested when I offered to let him use my cleaning equipment.

If I seem to be finding fault with the fellow's methods, I am not. He happily did not suffer my sensibility. The ugly grooves his gun barrel acquired from twisting wire meant nothing to him. A nick in my own gun seemed the equivalent of a wound in my body; there'd be scar tissue the rest of my life, I felt.

When I drove dogs on winter wilderness trips and returned to my cabin, I put them in a fairly large chicken-wire enclosure where they could run freely, and at night, go into their individual doghouses. They never saw the inside of my cabin, nor were they allowed to roam around the area to disturb wildlife. I have friends who spend much time in their yards, cleaning up their dogs' scats. At night their dogs sleep at the foot of the bed, not on the floor but in the bed. I am fond of dogs, but I have never had so amative an attachment as to kiss them on the mouth, to disregard their scats, tolerate their tracking in mud or scats on the cabin floor, and have them lick my fry pan to clean it.

Yet, I admit that if I could, I'd prefer to be less sensible, and suffer less fastidiousness.

The element of sensibility also enters in where rough

178

weather is experienced on the wilderness trail. I have known those who paid little attention to proper clothing, simply fighting the elements as though the punishment was required of them, when they could have been quite comfortable, properly clad, with rain gear or cold-weather clothing.

A rugged log-cabin builder was asked, rather invidiously, I thought, if his work didn't tend to coarsen him. "I suppose it does," he replied, "but it keeps me from becoming soft like a jellyfish." It was the appropriate squelch.

I suppose the low and high sensibility tolerance is a matter of needing a wide enough spectrum to encompass both fastidiousness and a pigging around—a gentility and coarseness.

Much of the abuse suffered in the wilds is, of course, due to a lack of ability to cope with it. The competent, sensitive individual tries to provide for every reasonable contingency. The sort of fellow who believes that he has to "rough it" in the wilderness is likely to make a mess of things no matter how tough he thinks he is.

The Pedal Reflexes

One of the most conspicuous differences between people who've spent a long time in the wilderness and those who spend most of their time in a city is that the latter have a reflex pedal problem on uneven, natural ground. Since he walks primarily on flat surfaces such as floors, sidewalks, and groomed golf courses, the city dweller tends to lose his stability when obliged to walk on wilderness terrain.

His long-developed reflexes, attuned to flat surfaces, bring about what might be called a pedal "blindness." That's noticeable even in the city where he leaves one flat surface to reach another flat surface just a step above or a step below. He's only "safe" when he can clearly see a conspicuous stairway. So common is this tactile blindness that we have court decisions determining if the need to watch where one is walking is the responsibility of the walker, or whether the step-up or the step-down type of construction in a public or private building is a hazard. Even a street curb often contributes to an accident. Many people stumble when they reach a curb, or fall flat when simply stepping down from a curb.

A resort operator posted a set of warnings in each cabin, stating that city people hiking in the area should be aware of uneven terrain. They were warned to watch their every step, in order to avoid accidents. This may seem farfetched and almost offensive, but a prominent doctor has reported in the media that we are virtually a "nation of stumblebums." Thousands annually trip over the slightest change of elevation or minor obstruction, spraining ankles and breaking bones.

Those who spend much time in wilderness areas gradually move out of the "stumblebum" element. They come to learn, as one famous woodsman put it, that every step in the wilds is of a different height, different length, and different quality, with as many devious hurdles and slippery steps. We need to develop a spring-step to avoid the flat-foot plod.

Does the wilderness-adapted individual watch the terrain to observe these differences? No. Just as the city man unconsciously expects every step to fall flat-footed on even surfaces, so in the same subconscious way the accustomed wilderness traveler develops a special tactility where the pedal reflexes operate independently of his thought and vision.

This tactility can best be acquired by wearing the kind of footwear that allows the feet to feel the ground. The Indian was a master in the art of walking in the wilds. He used the moccasin, with of course a great deal of wilderness experience allied to the natural development of his ankle and leg muscles. It isn't normally convenient to find flexible footwear—footwear that has a somewhat flexible sole, even though the sole is flat is passable. If flat, the sole nevertheless should be soft enough to allow at least a partial feel of the earth, and it should be light. Some footwear, such as the gum-rubber-soled "Wallabees" (a species of kangaroo), have a fairly flexible sole—an innovation sweeping the conventional world, giving the urban population, for the first time, comfortable, natural footwear. Their high cost has likely made them into status symbols. They look rather like moccasins. They fit the natural shape of the feet. Several firms put out what they call a rubber moccasin. It is well lined with fabric, has a gum-rubber sole, and a one-inch leather trim along the top, a short tongue, and a lace. Because they are low and well ventilated, they cause very little condensation in warm weather. They're as good a substitute for a genuine moccasin as you're apt to find commercially. The flexible-soled larrigan is sold commercially, too, but is getting scarce.

Thus, the city dweller in the wilds has to avoid the curse of his background—he is accident prone. Hospital records of great numbers of such accidents are stunning proof. Reflex development and hand and foot dexterity are now largely the province of the craftsman and the athlete.

181

Many vacations or holidays are cut short by activities attempted during the two-week stint—activities not a part of the urban routine in the other fifty weeks. Such time spent in the wilds can work a valuable emending process where the feet are reintroduced to the terrain for which they were originally designed. But we need to think each step in the wilds until the reflexes take over all their original instincts.

"Wallabees" and rubber moccasins

The Sacrosanct

Writers should often let sleeping dogs lie. In my book, *The Wilderness Cabin,* I treat at considerable length the log cabin tradition as well as its structural needs. One question I am never asked is "Are they warm in winter?" I hesitate to reveal the truth.

The truth is, most are not. Those log cabins made with jumbo-size logs—that have unusually thick walls—are fairly warm with average heating facilities, but cabins made of jumbo-size logs are rare. Cabins made with average-size logs need to be stripped on the inside of the walls, insulation placed between the strips, with paneling covering all. While one loses the log effect inside, it is retained on the outside, where it seems more important. One housewife complained that in her log cabin without paneling every log on the inside was a dust shelf. It's one of the realities of life; if you want romance you'll probably have to compromise with convenience.

Hunters are often assumed to have very educated taste-buds when it comes to judging wildlife as food. I am asked on occasion what meat I prefer; the questioner presumes that, as a writer on the wilderness, I'll show a special fondness for certain wild meat. When I reply that I prefer corn-fed beef to venison, tame ducks and geese to the wild species, pork instead of bear, on through the whole gamut, I offend his fantasy of the idealized hunter.

In early days when my canoe, dogsled, packhorse, and backpack trips extended into months of travel, or when I wintered in the wilderness, I often lived off the country. Wild meat served and served well enough in those circum-

183

stances, but proper feeding is the secret of fine meat. Even domestic cows that range in and out of northern forested areas give milk that is bitter, and, when slaughtered, provide only sausage meat that has to be highly seasoned to be used.

Some may say that it is "a matter of taste." The proper rebuttal to that is that deer foraging on domestic fodder in farming areas provide meat that's far superior to that of wilderness-fed deer. Hunters I know who have had the opportunity to taste both the "domestically fed" wildlife and the wilderness-fed, recognize this, but usually keep silent about it.

We need to see the wilds in its grand fidelity. The wilds have been the subject of faulty reporting for centuries. The wilderness needs none of our affected descriptions or fanciful distortions of fact. If we really "tell it like it is" we'll be astounded by the realism, magnificence, and genuine charm of the natural world.

Wilderness and the Hunter

It's difficult to consider the hunter and his relation to the wilds without getting into a psychological discussion of his basic character. Having hunted myself in the early part of the century, for subsistence only, while traveling in the wilds on extended trips, I could take either side of the argument.

There was a time when I was fascinated by ammunition, its trajectory and killing power; and by firearm locks. Had I then encountered proposed legislation to regulate or abridge the use of firearms, I'd have raised up on my haunches and given battle.

I used to consider my firearms the most attractive items in my cabin. Why then have I now given up hunting and hidden my weapons away? Because I have discovered that I was addicted to something that tended to seriously denigrate my broader and more profound interest in wildlife.

The hunter has made a strenuous effort to dignify his position. The picture is familiar: The open fireplace, a comfortable chair where the pipe is smoked while a retriever lies contentedly at his feet, a background wall of stuffed animal heads peering grotesquely into the room, an imposing gun rack. That's the conventional scene, testifying to courage, virility, and propriety.

The hunter is well fortified in his national position; the National Rifle Association sees to that. Hunters are a political force great enough to maintain the privilege of organized slaughter of wildlife.

What is more, he buttresses his position by arguing that he is instrumental in preserving wildlife. His license fees do this to a certain extent, but to a very limited one. He argues to preserve marshlands, but preserves them only so that he will have wildfowl to kill. He's not particularly interested in observing those fascinating creatures and their flight that graces the morning and evening skies. He doesn't appreciate this magnificent aspect of nature as a biological miracle to study, to inspire, to give life a profound sweetness; he wants to kill. Hunters must save wetlands to carry on slaughter. The culture must be one where wildness can be reduced to the level of the abattoir and still be conventionally respected. The tragedy is in the concept of slaughter for fun.

185

An oil painting that has common commercial appeal is not the masterpiece of marshland where ducks and geese swim and feed contentedly, but where a flock flies over a duckboat concealed in the rushes, shotgun blasts tearing into the flock, feathers flying, wings and legs broken. Sadism is here in a state of rapture. Slaughter has become a joy, but only to the sadist—surely a sad commentary on any boast of intellect.

The hunter argues that there is more wildlife (to hunters the word "wildlife" becomes "game") than before, suggesting that the kill of deer prevents overbrowsing. But farmlands have provided food for deer, otherwise the rapid encroachment would long ago have thinned them to a minimum or forced them into extinction. Hunters do not keep the herd healthy. They indiscriminately kill the healthy young animals while predators cull out only the sick and weak. Only natural predation helps to keep the herd vigorous.

Whatever we can concede to hunters in our most generous view, the whole fabric of the hunter's argument falls apart when we discover that few of them really know much about the wilderness and/or appreciate it. If he writes it is for hunting and fishing magazines. If he is the artist, usually his works are a bare margin above the level of the commercial draftsman, although he believes that they are immortal masterpieces. Like dead wildlife, impermanence is in every brush stroke, death lurking behind the easel to help enforce mediocrity.

A recent survey of hunters found that they were fairly good at identifying the creatures they kill, but have a lamentably poor knowledge of wilderness, campcraft ability, and survival methods.

I see no reason why a man should "outgrow his jackknife," but if he has the faculty to outgrow his addiction to slaughter of wildlife, he must have an inherent

186

"... marshland where ... geese swim and feed contentedly ..."

potential for intellectual maturity which he could develop.
I see more hunters of late laying aside their guns and
taking up photography, although I would be happier if
they didn't require any conventional excuse to simply go
out into the wilds and appreciate them. The pleasure of
enjoying nature for its own sake and learning something
profound about it should be ample inducement.

Through my writing I meet a great many people who
tell me of their interest in wilderness. I listen attentively to
what they have to say. When one tells me that he's a

187

hunter, I assume the kindly bedside manner of a psychiatrist, because I have found that little, if anything, profound that's based on wilderness observation will come out of his mouth.

Fewer and fewer hunting films get public attention, and those films that show the wilds, usually delete slaughter scenes in order to be acceptable. Hunters want praise. When they no longer get it for slaughter, we will have their help in preserving what wildlife we have left to enjoy. The father-son notion that they who slay together stay together is dying.

The Sadistic Fishermen

The practice of fishing all day with barbless hooks and returning the fish to the water so the fisherman can again have the sensation of feeling helpless, tortured creatures struggling for their lives on the end of a line, seems no less than sadistic. The barbless hook is supposed to denote an act of compassion.

One may be justified in categorizing the quality of human beings by how much sensual gratification they need to find life enjoyable.

In a casual conversation with some fishermen in Ontario's lake and forest country, one of the fishermen asked my partner and me if we were on a fishing trip. I explained that we were on a canoe trip and would catch a single fish occasionally and have a fish fry. One of the fishermen, clearly perturbed, asked, "What the hell do you do the rest of the time?"

"What the hell do you do the rest of the time?"

The Autumnal Transition

An experiment was made to determine at what temperature a frog would jump out of a vessel of gradually heated water.

The frog cooked to death.

In the same sense, many of us who live for extended periods in the wilds are surprised by the tolerance we gradually develop for temperature change. Here on this wilderness waterfront where I am writing, we had welcomed any cool spell as June progressed and merged into July and early August. At this latitude of 50° North, frost is likely to occur at night even in mid-August. So gradually does the cooling change come, one scarely feels the need to don a jacket. As an Indian friend of mine put it, "You suffer from the cold without knowing it,"—a contradiction that nevertheless describes how inured we become to gradual temperature change.

But late fall is not likely to allow this adjustment. Traveling by canoe in late fall—especially when using an outboard motor—often means dressing in winter garb. Living, as we do here, in a cabin on a thirty-five-mile-long lake, it is not wise to travel too far from home on a warm sunny autumn day without winter clothes stowed handily in the canoe. It might cloud up before noon, begin to rain, the rain turning to sleet, followed by snow and a howling wind. Even a blizzard is not unknown.

Early fall in the northern wilds usually provides the most comfortable weather of the year. Insects are gone and the heat of summer no longer oppresses. The prevailing weather is so perfect one would like to hold it in suspension, delaying the transition that comes all too soon when late fall merges into winter. John Burroughs described it as a condition of weather that makes you want to hang onto its coattails to keep it from leaving.

Yet there is a quality in the nippy chill of late fall that fascinates and stimulates. My Indian friend called it a "crazy time of year." By crazy, of course, he meant its unpredictability.

At this writing it *is* late fall. The wind is tearing at the lake while a driving rain thrashes against a northeast window through which I can observe the wild scene. A fire in an open Franklin fireplace stove offers cozy comfort. There is a feeling of having full command. In the wood rick, birch, spruce, and jack pine firewood is stacked to the top plates—firewood all of uniform size, ready to burn. Cutting, splitting, and storing it was not an unpleasant task. It is a late autumn chore that is zestful. A fragrance of sawed pine is in the air, and the dexterity one has developed in the use of ax and chain saw is manifest in the feeling of accomplishment.

One cannot hang onto the coattails of late fall, however, any more than onto those of early fall. Soon there will be a lacy ice fringe forming along the shore, followed by ice over the calm bays, progressing to an ice-cover over the whole lake. Wind will likely break up this cover once or twice, sending plate-glass-like sheets slithering from the waves far up onto the shore. Then a subzero night will come when thicker ice imprisons the water until spring. Not insulated by snow, it thickens fast. When the snow comes, the ceiling of the wilderness sky will seem more ominous than the summer overcast of an impending rainstorm. A few flying flakes of snow begin to spiral; they seem as if they can't decide where to land. This is but a prelude. The snowfall soon becomes more dense. Within the hour a white curtain has dropped, shutting out the opposite lakeshore, and the forest begins to whiten. You know that winter has come to stay until the sun brings another spring.

Then and Now

In the book, *Once Upon a Wilderness,* I sought to show how wilderness activity has changed from what it was in the early years of this century, and to show what it can hold for mankind in the future. Somehow those early years wore a pleasing quality; the elementary equipment and foodstuffs seemed more in keeping with wilderness travel than what we usually see now. Then one portaged a canoe with the tumpline and paddles. Food staples came in bulk; there were no packaged and canned goods; flour and sugar came in cloth bags, dried fruit in wooden caddies, bacon in slabs. For the trail all were packed in waterproof bags, then in packs that could withstand sieges of rain, or be recovered floating after a rough-water upset, leaving the contents dry.

All of this seemed so intriguing to some of my readers, that one wrote asking if I would, for a fee, set up a complete outfit, including provisions, that would simulate early travel equipment and methods. Looking back, I found that by periodic additions, I had come a longer way than I realized from the early travel methods.

A form-fitting yoke, contoured to fit one's shoulders for portaging a canoe, had replaced the old, traditional paddle and tumpline methods; a 67-pound, 18-foot, lightweight, Prospector Model, aluminum canoe replaced the heavy wood and canvas type that weighed 90 pounds or more when wet. Freeze-dried coffee; converted rice; potato flakes; powdered orange, lemon and other juices; powdered whole milk and eggs, freeze-dried meats, and a host of other processed foods had made food preparation in the wilderness much more expedient than it used to be and more savory.

Method of portaging the canoe with a yoke and with paddles

Nevertheless, those in the party of the man who asked that I set up the earlier equipment reported that in the five weeks of travel on the Hudson Bay watershed, both equipment and provisions of the old, traditional style seemed adequate.

We used to live partly off the coutnry, but then we weren't so restricted by conservation concerns and the need to save our remaining wildlife. I never liked to kill animals, and avoided it except when necessary. Some things gained, some lost—it has been a very tolerable compromise.

The Call of the Loon

The remoteness many of us seek is to travel for several weeks by canoe and encamp on a lake where only the people you're likely to meet will be a few Indians, Eskimos, or no one at all. With the camp made and food prepared, you relax in a reflective mood. The sun drops from sight. Dusk creeps over the wilderness, then darkness. Your campfire crackles now and then; otherwise there might be no sound except a wind whisper in the trees and the gentle lap of waves on the shore. You become aware of a faint glow in the eastern sky, a momentary suspicion of a forest fire. The glow soon becomes more pronounced, and you realize it is the moon about to rise over the water horizon. There it comes—red and spectacularly huge.

"Call of the Loon"

At that time you are likely to hear the most spellbinding call in the Northland—the loon. It will be as ecstatic over the moon's rise as you are. It seems to welcome the glow. In relay, several others will join in, sounding repetitively down the lake as other loons join in the chorus. Suddenly the hysterical call will cease and a long-drawn-out wail will follow like a foreboding warning out of eternity.

195

The first short symphony of the loons will strike to the marrow. One never forgets it. The sensation is that you're the only human being on earth or that other humans are light years away. If you called for help, you'd not be heard. The outside world is possibly over thirty portages away—a vague recollection of the return route is the best you can conjure up. An overwhelming silence creeps over the scene which you try to throw off by pepping up the campfire; at the same time the silence intrigues and excites.

Soon, wetting down the fire, you feel a wearying need to get into the sleeping bag. Now comes almost total silence, not even the crackle of the fire. You listen for sounds in the forest. When you're about to doze, from far out on the water almost beyond hearing again will come the loon's call.

And as you awake at daylight, and the day progresses, the call will likely be heard again, but it will not carry quite the fantasy of the call over a moonlit lake.

The Feminine Choice

When the eastbound Super-Continental, Canadian National train was sidetracked to allow the westbound Super-Continental train to pass at a remote siding milepost, it gave me the opportunity I needed to board it for Winnipeg. I carried my packsack of camping equipment after several weeks alone in the Ontario wilderness.

I wore a buckskin shirt, soiled by long use and weathered on wilderness trails; a felt hat from which I had removed the sweatband to make the hat cling in a wind; and an outer band made from a Montana rattlesnake skin. My wool pants by now were so assimilated to my body from periodical washing and wear, they seemed less a garment and more an actual part of me.

It was getting near dinner time and I was not only ravenously hungry, I had been looking forward to the change from trail grub to more fancy cuisine. But frankly, in my rough garb I had qualms about entering the diner.

Apparently the dining-car steward had seated rougher-looking men than I in his runs through the wild Canadian country. He placed me across the table from a very attractive, fashionably dressed young lady, whose attractiveness, no doubt, was intensified by my weeks alone in the wilderness.

I paused, standing for a moment, apologizing to her for my appearance, as though to give her a chance to frown on the idea of dining with such a roughly attired table companion.

"Please sit down," she said with a smile. "I like men with bark on them."

Crumbs on the Water Bring Back Loaves

That the St. Croix River on the Minnesota-Wisconsin border should be selected for inclusion in the National

Wild and Scenic River System is not surprising to anyone who has seen this magnificent stream.

We once lived in the Minneapolis-St. Paul metropolitan area, thirty miles away. We love unspoiled nature, and were not long in discovering the St. Croix. It was unavoidable that eventually we would come to live on the river. Our friends in the cities naturally found their way here to our St. Croix River fireside.

One morning, a good many years ago, a friend who was a regular visitor brought a young man who had a problem. As a student of electronics at the university, he had developed a serious nervous condition. With the highest standing in his class, he'd apparently taken his studies too seriously. He had developed a rather conspicuous nervous tremor, and it embarrassed him. His doctor had advised him to suspend all studies, and, if possible, get off into some natural environment for a while, one with less tension.

I was at the time, despite my varying economic circumstances, fancy free. I asked that he stay with me and while away a few weeks along the river. For six weeks with canoe and camp equipment we lived and traveled leisurely in the valley, until we became familiar with its tributaries, its springs, its flora and fauna, and natural enchantment along its one hundred-fifty miles. We arose each day with no urgency—as calm as the smooth flow of the river. The whippoorwill and the owl, the slap of a beaver's tail, the crackle of our campfires, and the muscial flow of the many crystal clear springs became familiar parts of each evening's camp. We lingered as long as we liked.

In a month I could see little of the tremor in my companion's hands. In five weeks, scarcely any, and he began to talk again about the university and his studies. I said nothing about his going back to school, lest he think that he was no longer welcome with me. At the end of six weeks, he faced the issue squarely. Much of his earlier problem was a fear that he would become a helpless invalid. Knowing that he could overcome his problem, it provided the courage he needed. He found a whole new attitude. He felt that he could go back to his studies with some of the nonchalance he had acquired around the evening campfires.

"I've no desire now," he said, "to become the electrical wizard I so avidly sought to be. This experience on the river has done more for me than settle my nerves. It's taught me the need of a wholly different outlook."

He did, nevertheless, become the "electrical wizard," as a research engineer.

Over the years I lost track of him and didn't hear from

"For six weeks with canoe and camp equipment we lived and leisurely traveled in the valley."

him until his retirement, some thirty years later. For convenience, he had moved into an apartment from a rather ostentatious home on White Bear Lake, a suburb of Minneapolis. Sentiment for his many personal possessions, he said, prevented him from selling them. There was a fine mahogany watercraft; a huge complex telescope; power, hand, and precision tools of many kinds; a substantial stamp collection. The detailed list of extremely valuable items would fill pages. Would I please accept them? I was to sell them if I chose, anything so that he would not have to suffer the sentimental qualms of a commercial parting with these long-familiar items.

The few crumbs I had thrown on the water came back loaves. More than the material treasure was the esteem that he held for me all those years and the memory of our weeks on the St. Croix River.

Vitamin C

Early explorers, spitting out their teeth, enfeebled or dying of scurvy through lack of Vitamin C, probably had passed many wild shrubs and plants containing this indispensable element. At this writing—September—our Canadian wilderness cabin camp area has an abundant crop of wild rose hips, one of the most generous sources of Vitamin C.

They make a delicious tea. The preparation is simple. Pick the hip (the ripened fruit of the rosebud) and nip off the calyx—the tiny leaflike tabs on the hip. This leaves a berrylike, orange-red globule about ⅜ to ½ inch in diameter. Dry the hips by spreading them out on a flat surface in the shade—not in the sun. When moderately dry, hang them up (about a pound or so) in bags made from ladies' discarded sheer hose, or net. In this second stage, allow them to dry thoroughly.

In order to preserve the greatest Vitamin C content, brew the tea below the boiling point. Boiling water destroys some of the vitamin. You can usually get three brewings from the dried hips: the first made quickly to the strength you desire. The second brewing made by soaking the rose hips overnight, and the third by soaking them over a period of about twenty-four hours. This last technique, however, seems to be stretching economy a bit far.

Most commercial rose hips come from European countries and can be bought in the organic and gourmet food stores. It's more fun and satisfying though if you gather the hips yourself in the wild and dry them at home.

Rose hips can be eaten raw to derive the greatest amount of Vitamin C; they contain many times more of that nutrient than does orange juice. If only the explorers who perished from scurvy had known about rose hips and other plants that can supply Vitamin C, how differently history might have been written.

A Time for Economic Wisdom

New York City's pocketbook at this writing is empty, and so is that of the little town of Buhl, Minnesota. They can't pay their bills. Both have discovered the mathematical fact that government treasuries are as finite as their wisdom.

It is time for all governments and each individual to recognize limitations and to plan ahead. There were times in my youth when, due to austerity, dinner consisted of hot cereal and milk for days on end. Hamburger was stretched only to make gravy for flavoring our potatoes. There were better times too, but in either event, bills were always paid, and they were paid because a little belt tightening now and then made it possible.

Not so long ago many wanted to acquire money to waste on frivolities. Pecuniary wealth meant abundance. The facts of life are coming home to us; goals are changing, and even the affluent waste less, save for a few disgusting voluptuaries who, even in the face of scarcity, continue as before. The considerate rich now turn out lights that aren't needed, and drive small automobiles. Not so long ago, it was fashionable to order a large steak and eat only a part of it. It suggested a kind of aristocratic epicureanism. Few will do that today. Nature is generous but has shown in its finiteness that heavy-handed greed has to be moderated.

Partridge Drumming

Of the many false legends of the wilds, one is a belief that the drumming of the partridge or ruffed grouse is performed by his beating his wings against a log. The accompanying photo shows this concept to be false.

Partridge drumming

While a partridge does use a log for his drumming, it seems to be chosen just as a vantage point, or perhaps to allow free movement for his wings in drumming. The position is interesting; he grips the log with his claws, then presses his sprawled tailfeathers against the log in order to acquire a firm, upright stance for the drumming ritual. The wings beating the air cause the low-pitched, muffled sound. It starts with slow beats, then a crescendo, after which the beat slows, and weakens until it becomes inaudible.

Like the song of the white-throated sparrow at eventide, the call of the loon over a large expanse of placid water, the timber wolf's howl deep in the wilds, the drumming of the partridge is another sound that lingers long in one's memory. It is now believed that drumming is the announcement of a territorial imperative, rather than a mating call. Could it be both?

The Bush Pilot

Most bush pilots develop an uncanny ability to find their way over wilderness areas, although few of them are acquainted with the more complex processes of celestial navigation. I've sometimes been mustered in to act as celestial navigator to find certain geographical points. One evening I had to be flown out of the wilderness a mere twenty-five miles. We encountered a storm and flew around the storm a hundred miles or more, entirely on the pilot's visual navigation which he accomplished with apparent easy orientation.

A forest fire—too deep in the wilderness to fight—needed to be located as a matter of record. I was flown with a pilot sponsored by the Forestry Service, and made some star observations to fix the position of the fire. Below us was an inferno. I asked the pilot what would happen if the engine quit. His answer wasn't encouraging: "Have you ever watched a poor camp cook fry bacon?"

A friend of mine was stalled for nearly a week in a wilderness area when a pontooned, bush plane suffered damage on a shallow reef. I didn't immediately realize what I'd said when I casually remarked, "Airplanes are not what they're cracked up to be."

Breaking Camp

For many years my wife and I have had to strain our indigenous bonds by going from one outer-suburban or wilderness residence to another. When many summer places are hot and insect-infested, we spend those months on the Canadian shore or wilderness islands of Lake Superior, where, near the water's edge, there are neither insects nor hot weather. We often experience two or three spring seasons. We enjoy our cabin on the St. Croix River early, and a second and even a third spring in the Far North as the sun's declination changes. Autumn also finds us in the Far North when August and September provide their most pleasant weather in the wilds. March is no pleasure in the northern latitudes. We sometimes hurry spring then by heading south a half dozen degrees. Early winter is fine, it's a period we don't avoid, but enjoy from latitude 45° on to the north into Canada's forest and arctic prairies.

I say "strain our indigenous bonds," because one builds deep interest, sentiment, and social ties in each locality.

Even in the cabin interiors of our various camps, the nooks and crannies to which we become accustomed are missed when we shift from one place to another.

In order to establish a kind of domestic uniformity in our living process in these cabins, we've made the interiors much the same, and placed certain items of domestic convenience in the same general relative places.

Four residences may seem an extravagance. I admit this is true. But writing, like any other occupation, has its own tools of the trade. The differing weather and geography of each place stimulates my mood.

And if absence makes the heart grow fonder, we have the delightful advantage of renewing friendships season after season. Internal tears are shed at the partings. We act brave and outwardly cheerful and talk about the rapid passage of time, but these are mere pretense. We suffer. The wisdom of psychology suggests that all of us should change friends from time to time. We fulfill this in a sense by managing to keep old friends and make new acquaintances by our itinerant shifts of residence.

What has happened during our absence becomes the first question when we arrive again at one of our places. Babies have been born to neighbors in the interval, people have died, mature trees that looked eternal have crashed to the earth and must be logged up for fuel—a funereal task. Younger trees, of course, have grown a bit bigger. Trails get a little overgrown in a single year and need some clearing, along with a certain amount of accentuating trail-tramping. Squirrels, chipmunks, Canadian jays, seagulls, and chickadees that fed from our hands the year before may be gone when we come back, but sometimes show up again, and before long regain confidence to feed from our hands.

Thus there is both joy and sadness in the coming and the going. I sometimes think about finding a place to live which is the best common denominator for weather, people, and environment. But, alas! no such place exists.

There is little education to be derived from traveling unless you can get enough roots into the ground you frequent, to feel the vibrant earth and truly know the people. Tourism is a perfunctory business which usually shows only a front—little of real value. Modern vehicles have value in getting us from place to place quickly, but speed leaves a cultural blank between departure and arrival. You need to get off at many places in between to visit, walk, or sit in deep contemplation, to discover intrinsic values. A concatenation of bus, train, plane, and ship stops allow no boast of having seen and felt the vibrant earth.

Squirrels return season after season.

In discussing the Canadian wilds, an acquaintance of mine said, "I have covered all of that territory." He had flown over it. I tested his knowledge of a half dozen rivers, lakes, and points of geographical and natural interest, then went from the general to the specific. He was acutely embarrassed. His scope was limited to the fuselage of his plane and the immediate locale of his landings.

Nor can I see that our having four places on the continent has provided us with any special advantage in covering a great expanse of territory. At best, they serve as hubs. Along the spokes of travel into the interiors there has been something to be learned. Those regions I have not yet traversed remain the greatest wilderness of my mind.

The Winter Wilderness

Those of us who have had an opportunity to travel in the winter wilderness by dogteam, on foot with a toboggan, by snowmobile and plane have found that it possesses interesting opportunities for diversion that are not usually appreciated by the average open-water-season camper.

Few realize that most of what is bandied about as characteristic of forest and tundra natives is not true. The Eskimo is popularly thought to be a blubber eater and to have other strange dietary proclivities. The fact is that the average city dweller eats more fat than does the Eskimo. In my book, *Paradise Below Zero,* I make the following observations:

In our tendency to be derogatory and facetious where naturalistic man is concerned, it may be a revelation to those who slurringly refer to the Eskimo as existing on blubber, that fat provides only a balanced part of his meat diet—about 1 of fat to 7 of lean meat and other foods—less fat than consumed by industrialized man with his bacon, fresh pork, full-marbled beef, butter, cream, milk, egg yolks, cooking and frying fat, candy, cake, ice cream, pie, cookies, suet puddings, and pastries. Since the fat in most of these exists in culinary disguise, the quantity of fat consumed is unconsciously far in excess of what is ordinarily realized (proportionately more fat than is consumed by the Eskimo.)

A rather substantial amount of fresh vegetable matter comprised the early and present Eskimo's fare. The gathering and drying of berries was and is common among them. A number of edible seaweeds, rich in minerals are used. A tuber called Eskimo

The friendly Arctic

potato along with plants of the vetch family are common and are prepared through the winter with meat. Some Eskimo tribes have for centuries consumed from 5 to 50 percent vegetables in their diet, all of wild origin. Now, of course, they purchase some commercial foods in those Eskimo-living areas accessible to supply posts. Thus, we can afford to abandon our disparaging concept of the Eskimo, along with a vast amount of other racial misinformation which we so glibly circulate for our own comparative exaltation.

Winter camping procedure today is most properly carried on with a double tent (an air space of from 1½ to 2 inches between the inner and outer fabrics), a lightweight, combination wood-burning and oil stove, depending on whether you're travelling in forest or tundra. The best sleeping combination is a light, compact, folding canvas cot that has a thick pad of down insulation attached to the underside of the canvas, rather than on the top, to prevent loss of insulating value by compression, a goose-down sleeping bag having much more down and loft (filling power) than the average sleeping bag.

Underwear is changed each night in order to dry out the suit worn during the day. This dried suit will be donned unlaundered the next night, and this method repeated daily. If a trading post, cabin, or other station is reached en route, it is wise to launder the suits, not as much for personal cleanliness as to remove the perspiration salt which tends to reduce the insulation value of the garment. One does not have to be fastidious in the wilds.

A duffel hood and a pair of duffel socks over regular wool socks should be worn while you sleep.

Where the sled dog is used in the forest, the toboggan serves best. On the tundra and sea ice, the sled, preferably with iced runners where possible, should be used.

In the winter wilderness by dogteam—the author and Indian companion on James Bay

If the journey is by snowmobile, it is wiser to tow a ski-waxed toboggan than the snowmobile trailer commonly sold. Should the snowmobile break down, the toboggan is easier to pull by hand. Moreover, the heavier and poorly designed snowmobile trailer will cause a heavier drain on your gas than will the toboggan.

Recently, some Indians and Eskimos have been turning away from the snowmobile, and even white trappers are returning to the dogteam. Two factors that seem to be causing this: the relative fragility of snowmobiles and the high cost of repair parts, as well as the impracticability and expense of transporting gasoline, very much higher in cost in wilderness areas. Dogs can be fed largely on trapline carcasses, fish, and inexpensive dog foods, made partly from bulk ground feed. Dogs seldom break down.

Indian Culture

Throughout my adult life I have been amazed how little the average person knows of the Indian, and how deliberate has been the effort to denigrate him. Here are a few words from the large Cree vocabulary:

Carefulness—*Yakwa'misewin*
Conscience—*Mitonā'y'échikun*
Surgery—*Muskikewe-kumik*
Science—*Kiskāyétumowin*
Inquiry—*Kukwāchekāmoowin*
Infallible—*Aka ka wunetotuk*
Considerate—*Kisawache*

Are these and thousands of other terms, equally erudite, the language of "savages?"

With the recent recording of the Navajo language, we have learned how subtle their speech is. They have at least

Handwrought items by Eskimos

ten ways of expressing many abstract concepts, such as honor and respect. Their vocabulary was originally recorded in their minds and improved from generation to generation—surely the most functional place to have it.

The Forest Primeval

The lumber industry has done an excellent job of convincing the public that reforestation is a great success, although the actual reforestation program is a lamentable failure.

An effort to get the lumber industry to cut only mature trees—the only possible way to perpetuate our forests—has failed. The argument they advance is that the cost of this method is prohibitive.

Therefore, the government has allowed the industry to "clear-cut," to remove every tree, to leave barren ground.

The lumber industry addresses this tragic condition with tree-planting programs. Pretentious laboratory experiments are set up to raise seedlings and plant them. This may seem to have the earmarks of good sense and conservation.

What actually happens is that only a small portion of the "clear-cut" area is replanted. Vast areas are left as open as a moonscape.

The cost of replanting is such that an initial $100 investment amounts to about $7,000 after interest has accrued by the time the seedlings have grown to trees sufficiently mature for cutting. Therefore, the replanting is often a front to mollify the public. Most often it is not, nor will it be carried out.

But assuming that clear cutting and replanting were carried out on all clear-cut areas, do we have a recycling program? Only for a very few generations of trees. The nutrients in the soil would then be exhausted, so that it would take a thousand years to replenish the sterile soil. We get back to the only solution; individual cutting of mature trees.

In its token experiments, the lumber industry has used commercial fertilizer with success. But success means spending more for fertilizer than the crop brings on the market. So, this approach fails, too.

Forests are rapidly diminishing as the clear cutting goes on, and the lumber industry offers token reforestation with great advertising pride and gusto. In the Boundary Waters

Canoe Area (BWCA) we have another lumbering tragedy. There the lumber industry seeks to clear-cut the forests, leaving only a hedge of trees along the waterfront. Where this is done, the wind blasts the hedge from two directions, laying the uncut trees down in a crisscrossed, devastating shambles.

We could perpetuate our forests if we cut the mature trees, but ravage seems to be a way of industrial life. We are told that the severe measures have to be taken in order to meet construction demands. This is fraudulent since a vast amount of our timber crop is shipped for greater profit to foreign countries.

The methods used in all of our resources have been to exhaust them as quickly as possible and get the money into the bank, or invest the proceeds in further industrial devastation of our resources. It has been heedless, unscrupulous, and avaricious.

Surfeiting

To be lean and hard suggests the need to avoid overindulgence. When we can acquire and provide a great many *things* we consider it achievement, but moderate consumption of food and material has proven to be wiser. Glut detracts from happiness and the optimum physical and mental life.

Comfort is a not-too-well understood condition. Most people don't hike because they find the thought of it and all that exertion uncomfortable. Obesity encourages more obesity because the fat find it uncomfortable to eat less, and highly uncomfortable to exercise more. The exercised, normal-weight, properly fed individual is the only one who knows what comfort is. Others are sick in varying degrees; that is, not optimumly well.

There can be a point where the biological and mental process changes. In my book *Paradise Below Zero* I have pointed out that when in the comfort of one's home there is a tendency during subzero outdoor temperatures to look upon the snow and cold as something to avoid. Yet, with the proper minimum of clothing for the hike and the existing temperature, after a distance of about two miles, there will be a physical adjustment. Your body will not only feel comfortable, you'll experience a feeling of physical and mental well-being from the exhilarating exercise. The indoor sluggishness departs, and the exercise imparts more real physical comfort than was provided by the lethargic comfort felt in the warm house.

At this point in a hike you experience a state of mind and body which you could not possibly have anticipated while in the warmth of the house unless you had previously experienced the invigorating process described.

Blizzards

DATE: November 11, Armistice Day, 1940. PLACE: Midwest. A rain began falling early in the day, changed to sleet, then turned to snow, the wind picked up until we had a howling blizzard.

Hunters were caught in the field, a large number of cars stalled on roads, workers were hung up in cities unable to get home. Few who were caught in the blizzard showed prowess in being able to cope with adversity. Twenty-nine people died in that blizzard, and many more lost limbs. People in cars tore out or cut up the upholstering from their car seats to wrap their feet, hands, and ears. Domestic stock suffered.

Most hunters proved that they were interested in game-pounds but knew little about the art of living in the wilds or of survival methods. A number of them died or were permanently maimed from frost bite.

Frozen pheasant—victim of the blizzard

DATE: January 11, 1975. PLACE: Midwest.

The blizzard of the century has taken place. Thirty-five lives lost. The November 11, 1940 lesson was not learned. Many people carrying on their daily lives today, happy, optimistic, confident of the future, will perish in the next blizzard, incapable of learning a lesson.

One wonders if this failure to cope with the unusual isn't true of nearly every facet of human endeavor. I came upon a crowd in the lobby of a building; they fumbled around trying to locate a pressure point to stop a hemorrhaging artery of a man who had fallen down a stairs into an iron rail and cut himself. The bystanders needed to know only the common Red Cross first-aid technique of applying pressure directly to the open wound until the ambulance physician arrived—they needed to put a cork in the bottle, so to speak.

No matter where a winter blizzard catches you in your car, you can survive comfortably. The technique requires no mastery of the elements, either. Along with heavy tread snow tires, put a small pack in your car. It should contain a pair of lightweight four-buckle overshoes fitted to a pair of felt socks, a pair of mittens, not gloves; down-filled underpants, a down-filled parka with a fur ruff, and a pair of snowshoes. This pack is life insurance. The addition of a down sleeping bag and a few candy bars or sliced and individually wrapped pieces of fruitcake can enable you to wait out a storm in your car if you're too far from shelter to reach it safely on foot.

A changing world requires individual initiative just as much as ever. What are now national problems might be resolved if each of us for our own sake, and generously for one another, were able to meet the average emergency without feebleness and dependence.

219

Our Greatest Poverty

No matter what our affluence, no matter how great our achievement, the brevity of each individual life hangs inescapably over us. *Time is our greatest poverty.* Early in life we tend to regard our fleeting hours as though they were infinite in number. Toward middle life we are generally caught in the earning syndrome; speculating, investing, scrounging, as though we thought we could buy immortality. The greater the dollar accumulation, the more certain, we seem to think, will be the immortal transaction. Late in life we look back regretfully on the accumulation of material and financial gain, wondering how much of our precious life lies waste in that pile, which in one way or another will eventually be dissipated, or increased to no avail by the same hours-of-life sacrifice.

The later years become the reflective years. Had we our lives to live over, those two-week vacations might have become long, repeated leaves-of-absence instead—times in which the most idealistic pursuits could be realized. The moments of daily stress, when near panic for results dominated our efforts, might have been replaced with periods of leisure, where compassion and magnanimity would have tempered a less noble course.

The conventional whip that was cracked over me earlier in life was not to waste time. It was time that had to be applied to material and financial gain. Hour after hour had to be equated with the earning motive, with industry, rather than self-improvement.

I deferred to my employer's every wish with honest effort and tried to give him even more each day than he asked.

When August came around, when heat and insects tapered off, however, I would take a leave of absence through August, September, and October.

My employer's reaction: "What's the urgency? Three months?! Wouldn't a week or two be enough?" Like the lemming horde rushing fatally into the sea, the industrial mass must move inexorably on.

I didn't offer an excuse for my absence. I simply made it clear that these were the months of greatest wilderness life fulfillment.

Certainly, one could not, I was told, run a business if employees capriciously ran off for months at a time "just to loaf." I agreed, but explained that I had a commitment to happiness that could not be preempted. One employer asked me if I was not literally "making a bum" out of myself. "No," I said, "I'll be living leisurely for three months just as someone else would live on a two-week vacation." Another told me that because of my "reckless leisure," he would blackball me so that I couldn't get a job in the city the rest of my life. I asked him if in planning to cut off my chances for subsistence survival, he expected in the process to stay alive himself. There were also big-hearted men among my employers. Several told me to drop in when I came back and they would try to find something for me to do. One in confidence discussed my departure with me at some length and later accompanied me on a canoe trip. Others seemed to envy me, but suffered in silent desperation.

A friend once asked me what I would do if suddenly I inherited, or was given (not likely) a million dollars. I would, I said, fit it as rewardingly as I could into the remaining hours of my life. Material possessions were not what I had in mind. What I had left over, which might be the larger portion, I would give away to others who richly treasured life's values and time, even those who pursued the arts in garrets.

221

Having only one dollar and being compelled to spend it, one might, as a great American once said, "Spend it as though it were a leaf and you were the owner of boundless forests."

My mother had a different pecuniary philosophy. She said, "If you have only a nickel, save a penny of it." That advice was given to me in my callowest youth. Since that time I have never been broke—nor, and fortunately, I honestly believe, not very rich. Had I been, these pages might not have been written. I might have been more eager to increase the pile.

My mother might also have given some other valuable advice, "Don't sell any more of your precious hours for dollars than is absolutely necessary; for beyond that, at any price per hour, you will be badly cheated."

Is it not strange that our greatest national economic problem is that we have ten million idle people? They want to give some relief to those who are employed too many weary hours each day and too many days each week. But we don't have the wisdom to give the employed a little more leisure by dividing employment with the others. If it takes nine men eight hours to dig a trench, while the tenth sits idly by and collects wages, is it not rather elementary that ten men could dig the trench in less than eight hours, with fewer backaches?

One of the problems in employing Indians is that most do not want to work full time. I asked an Indian why. The answer was brief: "White man is money crazy."

An Indian was asked why he worked only three days each week while others worked five. "I couldn't make it on two," he said.

Mobility

In my book, *North American Canoe Country,* I state: "Explorers, newly arrived on the coast of North America, exclaimed in their first reports to Europe: 'We can travel at will in the interior with the craft of the savage.' "

Last fall I stood on the shore of Saganaga Lake, a fourteen-mile-long body of water in the BWCA (Boundary Waters Canoe Area) between the United States and Canada. The lake is accessible by road over the Gunflint Trail, and a blacktop ramp allows the launching of fairly large displacement craft into its water.

I was visiting with some Indian friends of mine from Hudson Bay whom I had not seen for a year or more. We stood beside their canoe, to which was attached a small, one-horsepower motor—the so-called "eggbeater." Within the canoe were three loaded Poirer packsacks, mellowed by weather.

As we visited, a car and boat trailer with a luxurious craft and an eighty-horsepower motor was backed down the ramp, an elaborate mechanism having been provided for easy launching.

The owner, apparently enamored of his craft and obviously hoping to get the admiration of those of us standing about, looked somewhat down his nose at the tiny motor and canoe pulled up on the shore nearby; he remarked rather amusedly, "Where does anybody expect to go with that outfit?"

His cumbrous, luxurious craft would be confined to the immediate lake. Beyond would be portages which it could not make.

"We can travel at will in the interior with the craft of the savage."

My Indian friends, remaining mute, looked at me with an amused smile.

"I don't know where my friends here plan to go from Saganaga," I said, "but they just came about seven hundred miles from Hudson Bay by lake, river, and portage, with what you referred to as 'that outfit.' "

I refrained from asking him where he expected to go, but I was tempted to suggest where he might go.

Two men—one a philosopher of sorts, and the other, traveling salesman—sat side by side in a modern, supersonic passenger plane. They exchanged views. Said the philosopher, "This giant vehicle of the skyways—how wonderful it seems. Do you realize where it is going? Someday it will be dust. Where, after all, are any of us going?"

Said the salesman, "Do you mean me? I'm going to Omaha, Nebraska."

Dichotomy of Opinion

In 1919, when I lived in a cabin on the Flute Reed River, near where it empties into Lake Superior, I was asked by a tourist from Chicago if I would guide him to where he could see a moose. He didn't want to shoot it, he said, merely see it; and, if possible, photograph it. He spoke so reverently about preserving wildlife, I found him a very agreeable individual to visit with and escort.

The most likely place at that time and in that region was a salt lick about six miles back in the forest. No trails led to

225

Moose at salt lick

it, except the so-called "game trails." We saw not only one moose but several—a bull, a cow, and a calf.

I was so impressed by this individual because he only wanted to see, not shoot, a moose, I later spoke frequently about him. Then one day I received a package from him. When I opened it I found a fancy-stocked, high-powered rifle. Was this not inconsistent?

Had he seen the modest gun rack on the wall of my cabin and thought that I might be perplexed at his not wanting to shoot a moose? Did he want to show his broadness of view?

My wife and I are teetotalers. One evening while entertaining, some guests asked just before dinner to be excused so that they might step outside and view the natural surroundings here in the river valley. I learned later that they had gone behind a cache building and taken a swig or two from a hip flask. They didn't want to offend my wife and me with their drinking. When they returned and sat down to dinner, they found at each of their plate settings a Scotch highball. I somehow was reminded by it of having received a gift rifle from an apparent wildlife conservationist.

Economic Security

When in the Canadian winter wilderness I came upon an Indian family—father, mother, and young son—living in a

"I came upon an Indian family in a tepee."

tepee, I was intrigued by the ingenious construction and function of the shelter. At the same time I felt a bit sorry that Indians had to be reduced to such means. But should I have been?

I was congenially received into the warmed sixteen-foot tepee and given a meal of caribou steak, wild rice, and sauce made from dried berries and maple sugar. My sled dogs were fed by them and tethered in the nearby forest, protected from the wind.

The family had a good supply of various wild meats and fish on hand, vegetables from a small garden patch, wild rice from the river, dried wild berries of various kinds, and some cash—proceeds from a trapline.

It occurred to me that if the conventional, urban family had a home that did not cost them anything, except a little healthful labor, no mortgage, no taxes, no fuel costs, a tiny food bill, no water bill to pay, no transportation costs, no recreational costs, and little or no medical bills; whatever that family earned by salary or income would place them on a relatively high economic level.

What was most significant as I visited overnight with this family was an absence of tension, an unforced amiability, apparent happiness, and contentment. The young Indian lad did not seem to have the conventional toys to play with, yet he seemed to have an avid interest in his surroundings in and outside of the tepee, and in whatever was going on. When I gave him a jacknife that I had carried and did not need on the trip, since I had a sheath knife, he was ecstatic, and took it to bed with him. By having less, he had apparently acquired a sense of values and an environmental consciousness.

Iced Runners

Industrial man has no corner on ingenuity; necessity became the mother of invention ages ago. The Indian and the Eskimo have applied principles in the making and use of their equipment which show extraordinary powers of observation and an ability to wed them to their needs. One outstanding instance is the mudding and icing of their sled runners. If wood sled runners would slide readily over snow and ice, the early native must have reasoned, would not ice runners slide even more readily over ice and snow?

But sled runners could not be made of ice alone and endure. Icing the wooden runners did not prove satisfactory, since ice would not satisfactorily adhere to wood. But it was discovered that mud adhered tenaciously to wood, and ice as tenaciously adhered to mud. Mud, therefore, became a sort of catalytic bonding agent, an intermediary to solve the problem.

Ordinary mud was not practical, but the peatlike mud that came out of swamps was ideal for the purpose. Mixed with water, it forms a "dough," which is applied to the wooden runners as shown in the illustrations.

After being roughed on with the hands, the mud is subsequently smoothed with a carpenter's plane, in more primitive times with rough and smooth rock, and then iced with a cloth pad and water, preferably with a piece of polar bear skin with the hair on. Heavy loads are readily pulled with such ice-runnered sleds. Sled travel is greatly facilitated since one needs to use and feed fewer sled dogs.

231

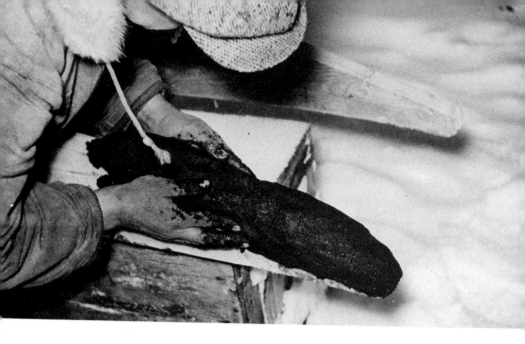

Mudding and icing sled runners

The Variable Wilderness

We tend to believe that anyone who's become thoroughly acclimated to one environment will not fare too well in a wholly different setting—one with different terrain, temperature, and the like.

Peary's companion on his expedition to the North Pole was Matt Henson—a Negro. I once had a companion on a Manitoba canoe trip who called himself a former "desert rat." He found that the forest, lake, and river country provided such a bounty in water, fuel, and such a comfortable temperature, he thought it an unbelievably luxurious environment. He did, however, suggest that the desert could use some of the excess when one leg of our journey was rained on, virtually without letup, for five straight days.

When I was asked by a Minnesota college to set up an expedition to the Falkland Islands, I asked, "Where are the Falkland Islands?" They didn't care that I didn't know where the islands were. My host presumed that whatever of wilderness living and travel techniques I had developed would apply there. In preparation, I learned, among other things, that the wind on the Falklands blows continuously at no less than twenty-five miles per hour. A gasoline stove would therefore need specially designed and fitted windbreaks. The tents would need to be of a shape to withstand winds. They'd have to be easy to pitch in high winds, too. I found that my own versatile equipment and methods could be easily modified to suit the elements and terrain.

When I had learned where the Falkland Islands were, I read everything about them I could get my hands on. Over

233

this theoretical knowledge, I superimposed several decades of practical experience gained in the wilderness in many parts of the North American continent. And although I'd never been there, the specifications which I drew up for the Falkland Islands expedition worked; the expedition succeeded.

Then it occurred to me that that's the way virtually all exploration into unknown lands had been planned throughout history. No matter what we attempt, we first need to set up a theoretical basis. For example, in the computations of celestial navigation for position finding, we assume a position and work the problem. In the final calculation there will be an error between the assumed position and the actual position determined with a sextant. But when the extent of this error becomes accurately known, the intercept correction is easy to make.

My Wilderness Blunder

I had to blunder sometime. It had to come in the law of averages, even on that promising, flawless, beautiful, sunlit morning—every evidence that it would be an enjoyable day—a day that would reward any effort put forth. It was late fall and the temperature was crisp enough to freeze narrow, lacy fringes of ice along the shore. The wood fire in the open Franklin fireplace stove gave the cabin a warmth and cheer that made a leisurely breakfast a splendid delight—a time to speculate on what the day's agenda would be. As I fed the fire for the second time, I noticed that my wood supply was getting a bit low.

I collected ax, saw, picaroon, and incidental wood-gathering equipment, and placed them in the canoe. An island a mile up the lake from the cabin had a considerable amount of dry, downed timber, the wind having laid low any tree not well-rooted.

Where it isn't possible to draw a canoe up on shore due to the ruggedness of the terrain, it is wise to snub it up tightly against the shore, using painter ropes at both ends of the canoe. Because the shore was so steep where the wood lay, I was only able to secure one end of the canoe. Some aluminum canoes have tying links made from stamped out metal; so did this one. The hazard here should have been apparent to me, and to the manufacturer; since the links on this canoe had sharp edges that could cut painter ropes like a knife. With my blind faith in industry, I overlooked that fact.

I worked on the island bucking up wood, making several trips to the canoe. When taking the last load to the canoe, I found that the canoe had cut itself loose and was floating out on the lake, an offshore wind carrying it away. I had the wood-cutting tools on the island, which I could have used to build a raft. In the interval, had I taken the time, the canoe would be carried along by the wind until I would have little chance of catching it with a sluggish raft and only a pole for a paddle.

I could catch the canoe by swimming after it. Stripping naked, I made a flying surface-dive and hoped that when I reached the canoe I could get into it and paddle it back to the island.

As I reached the canoe, I found that I would upset it if I tried to get into it with its heavy load of wood. To unload it piece by piece would keep me in the icy water too long, risking cramps. Since the wind was too strong to push the canoe back to the island, I continually pushed it, and then swam after it toward the nearest downwind shore. By the time I reached land, I had suffered considerable exposure. I was barely able to crawl up on the rather rugged shore. I knew that I had to keep very active. Emptying the canoe and beaching it, the activity got enough circulation back into my body to allow me to get into the canoe and paddle it toward the island.

When I came within a quarter-mile of the island where I had been gathering wood, a canoe with two Indians—a man and a woman—passed within calling distance. I called out while paddling furiously. They seemed amazed, and offered no response. I stood up in the canoe, calling again. Did they consider me insane, standing naked in a canoe in this weather, my genitals exposed to the woman, or did they regard me as the "Windigo"—"the man in a canoe who eats Indians, one at each meal?" They exchanged quick glances between themselves and then paddled off with rapid strokes, not even looking back.

Perhaps under the circumstances, they could not have helped me any more than I could help myself, but it seemed at the time that I could use some back-up aid.

Once back on the island, I got into my clothes as quickly as I could, then paddled fast for my cabin a mile away. I raised the temperature of the cabin to its maximum. I drank as many hot drinks as I could hold, filled my stomach with warm food and crawled into a down sleeping bag. It was several hours before the numbness completely left my body. A deep feeling of congestion hung in my lungs for about twenty-four hours, but I managed to stave off pneumonia.

It's not difficult to see the lesson in the old parable of the loose nail in the horse's shoe. Had the canoe manufacturer understood that leaving sharp edges on a canoe towing link could mean death, perhaps he would have sacrificed a nickel of additional profit by dulling the edges. Or would he?

The Indomitable Natural Force

I'm going to end this book on an optimistic note because I *am* optimistic. Nature is here to stay. Wildness is here to stay. It has been and will continue to be the "preservation of the world." Of that I feel most certain. But my optimism does need to be qualified.

Nature recycles plants and animals, including humans. Decomposition is a part of that process. When the overwhelming spectacle of a steel arch bridge is finished, the painting crew works year in and year out to keep its oxidation from crumbling it into the earth. When the crew gets it painted, they go back to the starting point and paint it again and again in perpetuity, generation after generation.

And so it is with all of our artifice. If we don't maintain it, eventually it will crumble to earth where in the recycling process, trees will rise and flowers will bloom where it stood. Manhattan Island would in time be what it was when we bought it from the Indians; wild, forested; Broadway a game trail. In the infinity of time, our most spectacular and revered edifices crumble into the soil.

When highways have their sharper curves lessened, it

takes but twenty years for the abandoned asphalt curves to send up trees and brush through the pavement.

I've flown over a vast wilderness in Canada. The wilderness is there, I assure you. A portion of the United States is still wilderness. If one could estimate the amount of growth, the amount of natural recycling that has taken place all over the world while I wrote this page, it would stagger the imagination.

Time is no factor where Nature is concerned. If the human species should by some catastrophe be eliminated from the earth, or vastly reduced in number, Nature would restore itself. The ocean, the freshwater lakes, and the rivers would gradually be cleaned up without man's help, until they were crystal-clear again. All the particulate matter in

Asphalt highway returns to Nature.

the air and the noxious gases would settle to the earth while the vegetation oxygenated the air to its norm—where it was before industry's ravage. Every edifice constructed by man would crumble into the earth, in time so obliterated and lost in the vegetation as to leave little or no evidence of a human race having existed.

Try to imagine New York City and other harbors of the world with no ships, no skyline except where the forest was contrasted against the blue, the air fresh, the Hudson River, for example, flowing crystal clear into an ocean of clear saltwater.

Consider then the gradual emergence of a human species upon that scene, a people sufficiently intelligent and technologically competent not to pollute the ocean, fresh waters, and the air—a race highly conscious of the finite nature of resources—men who understand the indispensability of wildness for their survival—beings who appreciate quality, beauty, and durability in whatever they fabricate so as to maintain a clean environment by not making a hundred shoddy items that are planned to become obsolete where one permanent article would do—a race that had the courage and rationality to keep its own numbers limited to where the world was kept viable for all life—a race where greed and willingness to ravage were not considered civic virtues, where such violations and indiscretions brought only shame and penalty—a race that understood clinically and psychologically the need for leisure and studious observation—a need for health and happiness—a race that did not spend billions of dollars erecting places to gather for the purpose of socially perpetuating obscurantism rather than intellectual and moral enlightenment—a race that understands the brevity of human life and finds that the only way to enrich that life to its fullest measure is not to heap materialism on materialism in a greedy orgy of futile self-indulgence, but to live magnanimously and

241

nobly so that fellow creatures can respect one another.

A millennium?

Not at all.

We are working in that direction, stumbling slowly along, but working at it, making our share of mistakes, but almost imperceptibly inching our way.

And so is Nature working at it. While man ravages, Nature slowly, constantly undoes our worst. We're seeing the first stirrings of human intelligence that will manage its society and existence in a way that civilizes, although generations may pass before it emerges completely.

The problem is not the failure to understand ecology or that the plundering of our resources can destroy the viability of a wholesome world forever. It can't. It can only retard nature's restoration process, degrading life until we learn. It becomes a matter of housekeeping. We are dirtying up the environment which we need to leave clean in order to live in dignity. Where we needed, euphemistically speaking, to forage lightly, we are rooting like penned-up swine, and wading in our mire.

The tragedy is that this generation, and we don't know how many more, will have to wade in that mire before we learn to live wholesomely.

But Nature is patient. The three billion people on earth will pass in the flick of Mother Nature's finger; other billions, more or less, will take their place, recycling the elements of past generations over and over again to create new generations. It is as though a single individual is of no more significance than a grain of sand on the ocean's shores.

How many such generations will pass before the accretion of knowledge will reach a state where the term "civilization" carries its original intended connotation? Are we to carry on so slowly with the process of restoration that progress will be only barely apparent? We could go faster.

We could accrue benefits for those who live now.

Many among us are bent upon hampering every phase of Nature's restoration work. But these plunderers are worried, because more and more people have discovered that human values are not to be measured solely in dollars. They are advancing over the horizon like the early morning glow of the sun; their number is growing. In time they will be legion. They are beat down by those who would ravage the earth and bank the proceeds. But they rise and keep coming, indomitably.

There is enough remaining wholesome earth to save. There is enough remaining wholesome earth to enjoy. The pendulum may not be swinging toward a condition where Nature is getting cooperation enough to promise a viable, early, future existence, but the pendulum which has been swinging wildly for years in favor of the greedy is slowing down. At times one even senses that it has stopped and might any moment begin to swing the other way.

Wilderness enough to be the preservation of the world still exists. We can enjoy it today and save it for coming generations. Invite them to a clean, unspoiled world. If we do, they will want to know about us. That is real immortality. But if we don't leave our descendents a habitable life-affirming world, we'll deserve to be forgotten, and in their willingness to forget would be our eternal death.

"Invite them to a clean, unspoiled world."